It Takes a Brigade

TWENTY-TWO A DAY MINUS ONE,
I AM THAT ONE

Maria Gastelum

TRILOGY CHRISTIAN PUBLISHERS
TUSTIN, CA

Trilogy Christian Publishers
A Wholly Owned Subsidary of Trinity Broadcasting Network
2442 Michelle Drive
Tustin, CA 92780

For information, address Trilogy Christian Publishing

Rights Department, 2442 Michelle Drive, Tustin, Ca 92780.

Trilogy Christian Publishing/ TBN and colophon are trademarks of Trinity Broadcasting Network.

For information about special discounts for bulk purchases, please contact Trilogy Christian Publishing.

Manufactured in the United States of America

10 9 8 7 6 5 4 3 2 1

Library of Congress Cataloging-in-Publication Data is available.

ISBN 978-1-64088-639-1

ISBN 978-1-64088-640-7

Contents

To my daughter Tatiana Shellman

Acknowledgements

To my parents, Aristeo and Maria J Gastelum, and daughter, Tatiana Shellman.

My siblings, Aristeo Gastelum, Jesus Gastelum, and Leticia Santos- Gastelum.

Pastors Sam and Tina Quiocho, Lilli Alcala, and my family of Victory Outreach East Phoenix

Transition to
Civilian Life

I had suffered a great loss, my army career ended due to a military sexual assault. And it didn't end pretty because my mind didn't feel beautiful at all. After a several months of emotional abuse from my brigade, I finally was granted authorization to exit the entire tragedy of a life that I had been living for the past five months!

I finally got in my Chevy 2004 Malibu and viewed Ft. Riley from my rearview mirror. It was about time to say goodbye to all the troubles that had crept into my life the past three years that I had been here. Now I was free to leave this post and live my life. It was Thursday May 5, 2005 and I was on my way southwest to visit my friend in New Mexico.

After driving for several hours from Kansas I arrived in Albuquerque, on May 5, 2005 and checked into a hotel to spend the night. The next morning, I was well rested and prepared to go back on the road to visit my army veteran friend Emma Brown Feathers who lived near Gallup, New Mexico.

Emma met me at a restaurant for lunch then I followed her to her hometown in Gallup. She wanted to take me to a place where they sold tamales. We made a big deal about finding good tamales because not everyone makes them with the same ingredients. These were very good tamales, and she proved me right when I tasted the first one. All those times when we were in Iraq when she mentioned these delicious tamales. I could just taste them and then it actually happened.

I spent a short time on her reservation near Gallup. Emma showed me around her town and introduced me to her family. I also was honored to meet her grandfather, who was also a veteran. I was so excited because my desire came to pass to meet the people and place she spoke about during our deployment to Baghdad, Iraq. I was filled with joy to have personally seen her hometown, and after meeting some of her family, I continued with my permanent move to Arizona.

It took about another five and a half hours to arrive in Phoenix. I wasn't sure what side of Phoenix I had exited off the freeway, and I was going to call my sister to let her know where I was. Then I saw some people walking in front of my car, so I asked then where I was. A young girl answered and told me that I was at Van Buren and 27th Avenue. Since I wasn't familiar with the Phoenix area at all, I called my sister and told her my location. She sounded startled and said, "Be careful, there's hard core criminals in that area". I told her not to worry about me because Jesus was with me. I went on to say that everyone seemed friendly to me, and no one looked like they were going to hurt me. As I continued to drive north on 27th Avenue, I found the street where I was supposed to turn on to get back on the freeway to continue on to my sister's house. Some minutes later I arrived at my destination and was welcomed home by my mother and the rest of my siblings, my niece and nephew, and my former sister-in-law.

I was missing that structured family life. There was so much to do to become a civilian once again. One of the first tasks was to search for a job because I was out of an income. I waited until the next business day, which was Monday May 9, 2005. That day I visited the nearest Phoenix unemployment office to apply for my benefits. It was at this office that I found out from the person who assists veterans that I could get compensation for bodily damages while serving in the military. This gentleman was very kind to me, and he gave me the address and phone number of the Phoenix Veterans' Administration Regional Office where I could apply for benefits. I did as he recommended and, within a few months, I began to receive disability compensation.

The next place for me to visit was the Phoenix V.A. Hospital to enroll for medical services. I walked to the information desk and asked to be directed to the ID office where I was given a number to wait for my turn. Within minutes I received my Phoenix V. A. Medical ID Card and had access to medical treatment at the hospital. I needed to enroll in some psychiatric treatment for Military Sexual Trauma (MST). The pain of being assaulted was troubling me deeply and keeping me hostage from being what God had created me to be. Although I didn't want to re-live the experience all over again by having to explain in detail what happened to me in January 2005. I knew that I had to talk about it to all those who needed to know.

After I enrolled at the Phoenix V.A. Hospital and received my initial intake as a patient, I was directed to the Phoenix Veteran Center because I had been in combat and qualified for the services rendered to all war veterans. The Phoenix Vet Center was the first location in Phoenix where I saw a professional regarding my MST. In the beginning, I was given a document to complete, and I had to answer some questions to the therapist who was interviewing me. Once all that was accomplished, I was assigned a counselor for my traumatic experiences in the U.S. Army.

It wasn't long after I had processed through the hospital that I was sent to the rating doctors for my compensation. I was questioned by the medical team that evaluated every veteran who goes through the application of compensation for injuries and illness that were initiated or aggravated during the veteran's time in service. This process reminded me of my days during my enlistment to the army. It was a very similar experience. The medical examination included both physical and mental, but this time it was to determine qualifications for monetary compensation.

Education

While I waited to hear from Veteran's Affairs regarding my application, I continued with my transition into civilian life. I had some goals that I had set for myself as a resident of Arizona, and one of them was to enroll in college to finish my bachelors of science degree in Biblical Studies.

I did my research on various colleges and universities that Arizona had to offer in the Christian/religious community. I found one that met my needs and I inquired about the bachelor's degree program in Biblical

Studies. Wayland Baptist University of Plainview, Texas had a site in Phoenix and one in Glendale at Luke's Air Force Base.

I made an appointment to meet with a professor, Mr. Paul, of the university who was going to assist me with my complete application process for the degree program at WBU Phoenix Campus. He brought me a packet of information about the program I was interested in and an educational plan for me to follow as I completed the required courses of my degree choice. Within a couple of weeks, I was a student of WBU. I wanted to finish my degree at an accelerated pace, so I also enrolled at a Maricopa County Community College to meet all my requirements for my undergraduate degree.

Deep Dark Moments

Everything in my life was going at a normal pace with the exception that there was something missing according to some individuals in my life who suggested that I seek employment. It was easy for people to tell me to seek employment, but it was difficult for me to follow through with their recommendations because, in reality, I wasn't ready to go back into the workforce. I was still in therapy and needed time to heal from my emotional problems that had become rooted deeply within my spirit and soul.

There were some things going on in my mind that I needed to sort out and get rid of. I had no way of explaining what was going on in my head and heart because I began to get anxious and got lost in my mind due to all the medications that the medical doctors had prescribed to me.

My body was experiencing excruciating pain that, on a level from one to ten, was a ten. I nearly passed out because of the debilitating pain. The pain would begin from my neck and then radiate to my lower back. There were days that I couldn't even get out of bed because I was hurting so badly; crying and praying for the agony to cease. In addition, I was having problems at night with body sweats. I would wake up twice in the middle of the night, drenched in sweat and would have to change my pajamas.

I spoke to my counselor she told me that it was MST and PTSD symptoms. It could've been a combination of nightmares, fears and the medications that I was on, but it was impossible for me to find out the cause of these night sweats.

Ft. Riley

Even though my family meant to help during my transition to civilian life, they didn't understand me as a war veteran who had been discharged due to a military sexual assault. The thing that was not evident to anyone was that I had suffered a huge loss. I had lost my dream to become a soldier in the most powerful military in the world. But not my calling as a minister of the gospel of Jesus Christ of Nazareth. That was not taken from me.

I couldn't believe what had happened to me and, at first, I was in denial. I began to have trouble concentrating and wasn't able to hold the position in the army that I had been assigned to do. I was no longer deployable because I was going through psychiatric counseling. The Army slowly discharged me with an honorable medical discharge. It wasn't the ending I wanted as far as my military career was concerned. I had planned on serving my twenty years and retiring with full benefits. Now I had to fight to receive an honorable discharge because my leadership was attempting to discharge me with a less than honorable discharge after being sexually assaulted by an Army soldier.

I wrote to my Republican senator at the time to let him know how I was being treated by the Army. I made it a point to inform him that my chain of command had been conspiring to get me dismissed from my military career with a less than honorable discharge. He intervened and wrote to my leadership at Ft. Riley, making arrangements to have me discharged with an honorable medical discharge.

My biggest feat during my discharge process was to have the strength to keep my military bearing. I had to sleep in my room knowing that this predator was not behind bars. Also, my leadership never made any initiative to separate us from being in the same company. It was torture for me to have to be in formation every day, especially when he was standing directly behind me. I just felt my blood boil and my thoughts were racing about things that weren't going to make things better if I carried out those thoughts. I often shared those thoughts with my therapist on post, and she just shrieked when I would mention to her the things that I thought about my aggressor.

Family and Work Ethics

I wasn't too involved with family affairs because it wasn't something that I was interested in pursuing. My main goal during my first couple of years from my separation from the Army was to heal physically and mentally. One of my biggest obstacles were the thoughts running rampant in my mind, and the nightmares I was experiencing every night.

Most of my family wanted me to just get a job right away,but I wasn't in a position mentally to be around people. I just wanted to have the option of making that decision on my own terms. I didn't want to feel pressured because it would raise my anxiety to another level. I didn't feel comfortable being persuaded into something that I was not ready to do. Although I was interested in learning because it challenged me to be a scholar. I just couldn't adjust back into the workforce automatically after being in the army for nearly five years. It was difficult to go back to work after going through a sexual assault.

After nearly four months of being reminded by my family members that I needed to get a job, I finally began to search for part- time employment, and I was hired by Army & Air Force Exchange Services (AAFES) in Luke's Air Force Base. I enjoyed being in a military community once again even though the minimum wage pay kept me humble. I missed my fulltime pay in the army and had to make some spending adjustments.

It was a good thing for me to work once again because it was something I needed to help me become reacquainted with society. At that point in my life, I was grateful to those individuals in my life who insisted on me joining the work force. In my family, it is encouraged to have a job or a career. We do not want any government assistance programs to become part of our heritage. In my family we always motivate each other to work or go to school, and laziness is not an option. Like that familiar saying goes, "If you don't work, you don't eat."

As an AAFES employee, I had access to the base and could enjoy making purchases in the main store, the Post Exchange. I had some privileges that were limited, but I was able to assimilate back into civilian life because I had some military connections while I worked on base. I worked there for only two years because at that time I was interested in teaching and had applied to work as a teacher's assistant at a local elementary school in Phoenix. I also was the school crossing guard before and after class hours. I was glad to have an extra gig to help me with the school supplies I needed to continue my enrollment in my Biblical Studies degree program.

Driving and Traveling

When I was deployed to Iraq to the Bulldog Brigade in Baghdad, I was part of a team that convoyed weekly to Camp Payne for medical supplies. Although I was no longer enlisted or much less in the war zone, I still feared going over anything that was on the road. It was an instant reaction to have a war flashback about driving around anything that was on the road that might be a potential threat to the troops.

While I drove around Phoenix and surrounding cities there were many occasions that I had flashbacks while I was driving and feared that anything on the road might be an explosive device. When that happened, I would simply drive around the object and keep on driving. But there were those moments when there were vehicles to my right and/or left, and I was in danger of hurting someone if I swerved my car either direction. In those situations, I would either slow down and move over to the next lane when it was clear or speed up and pass the car that was in my way.

I got lost around town driving and not knowing when or where to stop. Many times, I would just drive, and when I came back to my senses, I would find my way back home. I never shared that with my family because I knew that they wouldn't understand what I was enduring. In addition, they wouldn't be able to help me. My family is a military family. I have a brother who served in the army also, but he couldn't relate to my military sexual assault. Just like the rest of my family, they were all clueless on how to support me during my recovery time.

I felt so alone and isolated it made me more depressed than what I appeared to others. During this time, I desperately hoped that there would be a program for veteran families that could help them understand the many traumas we had been through.

A New Name

For several years I was using an alias and lived under a different identity. This was a decision that I made on May 31, 1996, when I became a Naturalized Citizen of the U.S. When the officer who was interviewing me for my U.S citizenship asked me if I'd like to change my name, I said that I did and gave him my new name. From that moment on I was Mari Lu Barrera to the world and identified myself as a new creation. It was a way for me to forget about all my past hurts and, by changing my name, I would be entering into a new life with a new beginning.

It was now 2008, and I was seriously questioning the fact that I had legally changed my name and didn't even pray about it and ask God if he approved of my name change. Then for some reason this time I decided to pray about changing my name again with my first and last name only and came up with the legal name of Maria Luz Gastelum. I felt God's peace when I asked Him, and He approved of it.

I went to the local courthouse and asked for the legal documents to change my name back to almost what it was when I was born in Mexico. It took a process of six to eight weeks, and I received a court date. I went to the meeting and within a couple of hours I became Maria Luz Gastelum.

Have you had to transition from the loss of a job, divorce or other situation?

What did you do or experience during this moment in your life?

1.

2.

3.

For no one is cast off by the Lord forever. Though he brings grief, he will show compassion, so great is his unfailing love. For he does not willingly bring affliction or grief to anyone.

Lamentations 3:31-33 (NIV)

Church Life

The only place I could be comfortable around other individuals was in church. I had been searching for a church to attend and participate in doing God's work. Since I was already involved with a worldwide movement, I decided to become a member of the nearest church to me.

I adjusted myself into an Evangelical church by helping out in the Children's Ministry. My passion for working with the preschool- age children started when I participated as a nursery worker while I was a member of the affiliated church in Long Beach, California, in 1996. I really enjoyed caring for the infants and toddlers while their parents were blessed during the services.

After being dedicated for nearly a year, I was asked to become an overseer of the nursery and I accepted my new role in the church. I was able to encourage some of the mothers who would drop off their children to participate in the ministry. We were always searching for more volunteers for our nursery because we lacked helpers.

It is important to belong to a community because it gives one a sense of belonging and also instills a purpose in life. Being part of something gives our lives meaning and dignity. I had been wanting to be part of a church community since living in Ft. Riley during my enlistment in the army. I had kept in contact with an affiliated church known as "The Outreach" in Phoenix because I was going to make it my home church once I was honorably discharged.

I had been serving faithfully for nearly two years, and I was promoted as a co-facilitator in the weekly Bible Study that was held at the Women's Recovery Home. I was asked to teach there, and then after a couple of months of being a teacher at the women's home, I was invited to teach at the Men's Recovery Home.

It was an honor to have the opportunity to teach God's word to my brothers and sisters in Christ, but I was still suffering from PTSD symptoms and kept that to myself because I feared that no one in the church would understand what I was going through.

I was also interested in joining a women's ministry group that was offered on a monthly basis at one of the sisters' homes. I really wanted to be part of that group, but didn't qualify because it was for a 40-plus age group, and I wasn't yet in that age bracket. I was invited once as a guest and got to fellowship with my church sisters and find out a little more about their ministry. I envisioned myself hosting one of these meetings in the future because it's important to bond with other women who go through the same life experiences as all the other female church members.

Intervention

I was very involved in my church, and it frightened my father that I was attending weekly church services. My family didn't understand I needed to find a mission to be a part of now that I was out of the army. I believe in selfless service; this is something that I learned in the army. This is a gift from God. He gave me the gift to be a selfless servant.

I worship Him when I serve others. I like giving of my time to help others because it makes me feel better when I know I have helped someone in need. I always look forward to assisting others in making their day better and brighter.

My father and his girlfriend at the time made a special trip from Long Beach to pay me a visit. I was so happy to see him but that visit soon left a sour taste in my mouth. Apparently, he was going to put a halt to my church attendance. This was not what I had expected the previous day when he arrived and was cheerful and having a good time visiting his children. It happened when it was time for him to depart and return to Long Beach.

As he walked to the front door, my father told me that I needed to stop going to church and get a job. He continued to tell me I needed to focus on my family and not on outsiders. I was shocked, but not surprised, when he said that to me. I was mindful he was still my father, but at the same time, I had to obey my Heavenly Father. Then he told me that my siblings took a good look at both of us because there was no telling how I was going to react. I was diagnosed with PTSD, and there was a 100 percent chance that it wouldn't end pretty. I was very transparent and responded immediately by letting him know he could tell me what he wanted me to do, but that I am a grown woman and I would not be obeying his orders. I had to remind him that I was not that "little Maria" who used to have to obey him. I continued by letting my earthly father, and everyone in the room know, that I needed to be in church and that I was going to continue attending church for as long as I had breath in my lungs. He could tell me all day long, but I wasn't going to obey his order on that subject. He didn't answer me back when I told him I planned on being part of a church community and no one was going to prevent that from happening. Then after several minutes of debating back and forth, he decided to end the conversation with me and left for Long Beach.

MIA From My Church

After serving about a year in the nursery and being an overseer, I was invited to become a teacher for the kindergarten-age students. Unfortunately, I only taught on two different occasions because I had a misfortune that caused me to leave the ministry. I soon fell into a deep depression and didn't want to attend church. I was wounded in the church. After nearly two weeks of missing church services, I began to visit other Christian churches. I still continued to attend Bible College at WBU and to work on graduating with my degree in Biblical Studies.

During this time, I met an up-and-coming preacher who was enrolled in several of my classes. He had been speaking to me about a prison ministry he was serving and invited me to attend one of the services with him and his team. He gave me a packet that I needed to fill out to become approved to enter the prison with them. Once I was authorized, I became a faithful helper in the men's prison ministry with this new team.

I also met a Christian lady who had become a very resourceful person. She invited me to her church for the women's Bible study. She shared with me that the class was reading a book written by a famous woman preacher who had her services broadcast through-out the world on a Christian t.v. station. I decided to make this new church my home church. I really liked the way that the pastor preached. He was always on fire for the Lord.

It was in this church where I received most of my healing from past hurts and failures that accumulated in my life. I became involved in the street evangelism that was part of the growing church. Many souls came through this church and got saved, delivered and set free!

Receiving Fire!

One day while I was at the altar the pastor prayed for me and laid his hands on me and began to speak into my life and said, "Fire!, Fire! " I fell back, slain in the Spirit. After this experience I became radical for Jesus. This pastor's words were so powerful to the point that it would transform me into another version of what God had created me to be. I wasn't ashamed of the Gospel, but I wasn't bold about it either. I had been lukewarm for many years, and it was time for a change.

Now that I had gotten hit with "fire" I needed to go back to my church to make my way back into my calling and purpose in life in God's kingdom. I had been praying about returning to the outreach, but I needed confirmation from God. After several months of prayer, the Lord spoke to me in a dream, and He approved of my return to the outreach but to a different one in the city. I slowly entered back into my church. The Lord told me to connect myself with V.O. East Phoenix, but I waited at least two months until I made the final move.

I had been a bit disappointed with God because he had taken me from a large church to an infant church. I didn't understand it at the time that the Lord was giving me just what I needed. I needed to grow up with baby Christians because of my problems with PTSD experiences and everything that I was going to go through as a PTSD patient at the Phoenix V.A. Hospital.

Once this small church moved to another location with a much larger sanctuary, and we all had some elbow room, the Lord began to change me I was gaining spiritual lenses and could see in the supernatural. God had begun to prepare me to use my prophetic gifting in a way that I could never imagine.

I was fine there at V.O. East Phoenix where the Lord gave me more use of my gift of divine healing. But He wasn't done with me yet as far as using me to heal others. Because I had been battling for years with depression and anxiety, He started to give me compassion for those who were suffering mentally. He wanted me to pray for those who were lost in their minds. In addition, He gave me more insight and prepared me to pray for those who needed limbs to be straightened. I didn't understand all these ideas He was putting in my mind, but I accepted what He was depositing into me.

It helped me to be a part of a ministry inside the church walls, and gave me ownership. The greeting ministry was the first one I began to help out in because I wanted to get rid of my shyness. I needed to get out of my comfort zone if I wanted to be ready for God to promote me into another level in His kingdom. Although I was still very depressed, I showed up to every service because I wanted God to heal me. I was desperate to receive my healing and deliverance.

Street Evangelism

During my healing process I attended church weekly and participated in as many ministries as I was able to fit into my schedule. My favorite one was street evangelism. This is when the church gathers corporately and shares with the community about the love of Jesus Christ and His salvation for those who believe that they are sinners and need a savior.

I participated in the street evangelism team that was active in the church. Evangelism was one of my strongest gifts, and I seemed to transition well when I was in front of a person who was interested in listening to what I had to say about Jesus and salvation.

Our church did a lot of outreach, and there were times when we had rallies in the neighborhood. The brother in charge of the evangelistic team was the one who chose the location, and the others organized the event. I was usually in charge of the face painting for children, while the rest of the team prepared to give their testimonies to the public. There were a selected few who were able to go around and minister and pray for the people who came to visit us at the rally.

During the month of October, we would have a harvest festival on the church property, organized by the committee. We had several booths for the children to choose from such as the dunk tank where someone would be sitting in the tank and someone had to hit the target to knock the person inside the tank. We would select one person to sit in the tank, and the participants would make three attempts to dunk that person. Then there was the ring toss where the player had to toss the ring and let it land inside the stand. Of course, the winner would receive his or her prize. The winners would take home a goldfish.

It was a blessing to see so many children from the community come to participate in the harvest festival my church had organized. We made sure that each child went home with a bag of goodies.

Bringing My Sewing Skills to My Church

I was very active in the church and because I have sewing skills my pastor had asked me to upholster some chairs he had purchased. I took on this project without having any experience in home decorating or furniture remodeling. I had the tools I needed to complete the task. I went to the nearest upholstery material store in Phoenix, making sure I had the exact measurements of the chairs. Then I calculated how much material I was going to need for this assignment. It took me several weeks to complete the project, but when I was finished it looked like a professional upholsterer had done the job.

I'm the person who would also sew the majority of the costumes for the church plays held on Christmas and Resurrection Sunday. I went to the local fabric store to purchase the patterns that I was going to need for each actor. I also bought the fabric and any notions that were needed for each costume. I never got tired of working for the Lord because it made me feel good inside to be a blessing to others.

Loving God But, Still Hurt

I was so deeply in love with God that I just couldn't wait until I arrived on the church parking lot. My heart was filled with anticipation because I couldn't wait until I went inside the church building. My desire was to be the first one to reach the altar for the morning prayer before each service. I was faithful in attending every service. I was there for all three weekly services.

I enjoyed going to the altar during service while the worship music was playing, and I danced unto the Lord the only way I could. There were times when the Holy Spirit was very strong, and I would just run around the church with a smile from ear to ear. I saw that some people were smiling as I passed by them. I couldn't contain myself because I was so grateful and full of joy that I just had to run. I was running because I felt free from any bondages and from negative emotions that had been present in my life.

Then, there were days when it was the opposite and I couldn't move an inch. For example, one day the Holy Spirit had arrested me, and I just fell down prostrate and began to speak in tongues. I was immovable, and I felt my heart racing and panting for God. It was one of those moments when I would feel like I had touched heaven. I had finally made it to His secret place where He reveals His mysteries to me.

Being a servant of God has really helped me and changed me inside and out. I take joy in seeing others succeed and realize their purpose in life. Being able to disciple other women has always been a goal and objective for me. But, because I was still going through my traumas, I wasn't capable of discipling any women yet. Because I desperately needed to get delivered from all the hurts and pains that I had experienced. I was still stuck, and God couldn't use me to His full capacity. Although I was experiencing God's love, I was still hurting inside and in need of spiritual healing. I needed God more and more each day. I had experienced going to the secret place, but I still was hurting inside.

Children's Chapel

By serving in the children's chapel, I was helped to become more patient and compassionate with those who came into the church. I really enjoyed teaching the three to five-year-old children. I had a curriculum I was given to follow, but I was given authority to change it a little bit to accommodate it to the children I was teaching. Because the attention span of a child so young is only several seconds at a time, I was creative as much as I could be. There were times I would use hand puppets, which would really get their attention.

Women's Church Convention Spring 2009

We also attended the yearly women's convention. This particular year was the time I was still feeling sick with a lot of back pain, but I went regardless of my illnesses. I made sure I took all I needed to make myself comfortable during this trip. I had all my medications, a heating pad and books I wanted to read on my downtime.

When we arrived at our hometown, Phoenix, our pastor asked us to give a brief testimony. I began by letting everyone know that Jesus will return and asked them to turn to John 20:7 as I explained about the cloth that had been wrapped around Jesus' head. The cloth was still laying in its place, separate from the linen. I explained to the congregation that in Jewish culture when something is set apart and folded means that the owner is coming back for his or her property. Then I began to ask everyone, "Are you ready for Jesus?" Are you ready if He comes right now? Then people began to turn to their Bibles and were actually reading the scripture I had quoted. After our pastor preached, there were many who come to the altar who I never thought would answer an altar call. That was the power of God. Even though it was just a testimony, it was what God had deposited in me to share with my church.

Women's Church Retreat Fall 2009

Several sisters from our church went to the retreat. I hadn't been to a women's retreat in my life; this was my first experience. I was moved by the Holy Spirit and was so excited to be part of this leadership retreat. When we arrived home that Sunday we all were invited on stage to give our testimonies. I began to speak about an experience I had at the altar and told the audience about when we were all encouraged to pray for one another. I proceeded to finish my testimony and voiced that I saw three sisters. I lifted my right hand and began speaking into their lives, shouting, "FIRE! FIRE! FIRE!" Then some women began weeping and falling in the Spirit.

Church World Conference 2015

I had purchased these really beautiful silver color heels I was going to wear the night I was scheduled to sing in the women's choir. These women had come from hurtful pasts. Some were in the church's recovery home and others were graduates of the home.

I had forgotten my shoes in the hotel lobby and rushed back after arriving at the Staples Center in Los Angeles. I was wearing a pair of brown flat shoes that were very comfortable. The Lord spoke to my heart and said I didn't have to worry because no one was going to see me wearing those shoes during the service. Then I arrived at the rehearsal for the choir practice before the service began. We were going to sing before the guest speaker preached. While we were practicing, a young lady from one of the homes saw my pretty shoes that were in the box and was admiring them. I had received several compliments on those shoes and was more con-fident that I would get noticed because I was placed in the center of the front row. The Lord reminded me again that no one in the audience was going to see my feet.

I went on and continued with the choir practice, and then we had a break. I noticed that the young lady who had complimented me on my shoes had had one of her shoes break. Then the Lord spoke to my heart and told me to give her my new pretty silver shoes. I debated with Him about it. I said, in my inside voice, but they were $20. I'm going to need that money. I ended up blessing this lady with a pair of beautiful silver shoes that matched the silver shawl we all were required to wear. I was left with a pair of comfortable flat brown shoes that didn't match my dress. But God told me that night I was going to need to be wearing flat shoes.

A famous world-renowned evangelist was the guest speaker. He gave his testimony on how he became saved through the testimony of his father who was in his bed sick when an evangelist came knocking on their door and prayed for his father. His father was healed, and he grew up to become one the world's most famous evangelists. Then he was going to preach on the Holy Spirit and Fire. I felt it in my spirit because he gave us the following scripture:

John answered them all, "I baptize you with water for repentance. But after me comes one who is more powerful than I will come, the strap of whose sandals I'm not worth to untie. He will baptize you with the Holy Spirit and fire.

Matthew 3:11 (NIV)

Once he finished reading the scripture, I saw some people who had been seated on the right side of the arena were quickly moving to the altar. A security guard stopped me and told me to go back to my seat, and I said that I would. But I tricked him, and ran to the altar. I'm sure glad I was wearing those comfortable flat brown shoes! Before I knew it, I was right in front of the altar and in the center.

Then the evangelist noticed that others were running to the altar and he asked our founding pastor if it was okay because he hadn't even begun to preach. As he's speaking, I got all bubbly inside and my organs felt like they were being tickled. I just wanted to yell at the top of my lungs and say, "Hallelujah!" But I had to be careful because I didn't want to get into trouble for doing that while the guest speaker was preaching. I couldn't contain myself anymore and out it came. I yelled from the top of my lungs, "Hallelujah!" The preacher said, "Let's do this how we do it in South Africa. On the count of three we are going to shake hell up because I want you to yell as loud as you can, 'Hallelujah' and you are all going to receive the baptism of Fire! He counted one two, three, and every soul in that arena said, "Hallelujah!" And each received "Fire!"

My Prayer Life

I needed to understand God at a deeper level, and I learned that required more time in prayer. When we pray to God we are communicating with Him. I began with fifteen minutes at first until I was praying for an hour a day. This took time, but when I achieved my goal of praying for an hour, it seemed like it wasn't enough. By this time, I had already been thinking about fasting again. It had been years since I had practiced my fasting and praying routine. This was something I had abandoned since my days in the army.

I clearly remembered I had been fasting and praying when I was in Iraq in the war zone. I organized a fasting and prayer chain in my company before we were assigned orders to Baghdad. I even fasted and prayed when I did my tour in Kuwait after the 9-11 tragedy.

It was now 2008, and I was not fighting spiritually anymore. I needed to pick up my weapons and start warring the enemy once again. I was allowing him to step all over me to the point that I didn't even recognize myself.

Prayer and the Brain

It's a plus when you dedicate at least twenty minutes a day to prayer because it changes the function of your brain. The brain grows more cells in the frontal lobe as a result of long exposure to prayer. The frontal lobe is where the brain conducts problem solving, self-monitoring, awareness of abilities/limitations, organization, attention/concentration, mental/flexibility, speaking (expressive language), judgement, initiation, inhibition of behavior and planning/anticipation, to name a few. In addition, changes to the brain also occur when the praying warrior engages in praying in the heavenly language (tongues/chanting).

Do not be conformed to the pattern of this world but be transformed by the renewing of the mind.

Romans 5:12 (NIV)

Mindfulness and Prayer

I had learned so many things in counseling sessions at the Phoenix V.A. Hospital during my classes for PTSD and depression. For example, "mindfulness" to me is like prayer. Therefore, I went back to my Christian spiritual basic training days and incorporated all that was taught to me at the hospital and used those tools in a faith-based manner.

What spiritual assignment have you participated in lately or would like to observe to strengthen your spirit and align yourself according to God's holy Scriptures?

What questions do you have about feeding your spirit man or woman?

This is then how you should pray:

"Our father in heaven, hollowed be your name, your kingdom come, your will be done, on earth as it is in heaven. Give us today our daily bread. And forgive us our debts, as we also have forgiven our debtors. And lead us not into temptation but deliver us from the evil one."

Matthew 6:9-13 (NIV)

Troubled Moments

There was a brief period during my healing process I experienced sleeping a lot and was always very tired throughout the day. I had plenty of medication to keep me still during the day and night. But, because I was sleeping for so many hours during the day, I felt like I was losing time. Yet, at the same time, there wasn't much I could do to receive the help that I needed to aid my situation. For some reason I hadn't found any resources at the Phoenix V.A. Hospital or in the community to assist me in the trouble that was weighing me down without the use of prescribed medication.

I wasn't too thrilled about being out in public but, because I was working, it was necessary. I was capable of assimilating back slowly into the workforce and into the community. I wasn't sure about my future, but I was optimistic about the things that would take place in my life. I could tolerate being around people as long as I wasn't in a large crowd. If I did find myself in a huge crowd, I felt overwhelmed and experienced anxiety.

During one of my shopping sprees at a local chain store, I was walking around and, suddenly without any warning, I lost my memory. I couldn't remember why I had come to the store. I began to have an anxiety attack because I had no idea what I was supposed to purchase at the store. Then I decided to just walk around the store to pretend like I knew what I wanted and started to look at items like I was really shopping. I put things in my cart to make an appearance. A couple of hours later I regained my memory and remembered what I needed to purchase at the store. I quickly selected the items, put the ones that I didn't need back on the shelf, paid for my merchandise and left the store.

I never let anyone know what was going on with me because I had a lot of fears and didn't trust anyone. I was afraid that someone would hurt me if they knew that I wasn't coherent.

Being an Extrovert

I was at one time an extrovert, but now I had left the war scene, I was the opposite. I didn't even want to be around people, much less speak to them. The only group of people I could trust were those who attended church with me. For some reason, I felt safer around those with a religious background. I understood what it was like to be a participant in Christian community.

It really bothered my spirit that I was no longer tolerant of certain people. I only wanted to be around those with whom I was safe. I needed to be in a safe environment in order to be vulnerable. Once I was vulnerable, I could start my healing process.

It took me several years before I found places to be safe. I also was a very good judge of character and wouldn't be trusting around certain individuals. I had trust issues that kept me from becoming an extrovert, the person God created me to be.

Public Appearances

At this moment of my life I didn't want anyone in my personal space, especially a stranger. To avoid crowds, I did my shopping at night at a store that was open twenty-four hours. I remember this seasoned woman was in line behind me, and she needed to pay for her items. She got in my personal space and I began to feel threatened. I told her to step back because she was too close to me, and it was making me feel uncomfortable. She wouldn't listen to me until I sternly told her to step back and get out of my personal space. Finally she listened, but by then someone had called security on me. It didn't matter to me because I was on hypervigilant mode and nothing or no one could get me out of this mindset.

I eventually calmed down and left the store and sat in my car for about fifteen minutes, reflecting on the experience. I worried because I thought I was losing my mind. I felt so afraid and alone. Soon I began to cry and asked God to help me because I was so lost I didn't know what to do. I didn't know who to turn to in my community. About half an hour later, I was feeling more grounded and proceeded to drive my car out of the parking lot and go home.

I didn't tell anyone what I was going through. There were no words at the moment to describe the torture I was experiencing. I felt like I wasn't living at all. I was simply existing, and the only way I could survive that moment was to be in survivor mode. I was familiar with being a survivor, but this time it was a different type of survival I had to endure. It was as if I was just a body with organs, but no feelings or emotions. I didn't know how to feel or react to people or various situations. I had become a very numb person because I was hurt.

Lost Track of Time

I would lose my memory plenty of times. On one occasion, I went to a mall to shop. I had no idea what was going to happen next. When I walked out of the mall doors I realized I didn't remember where I had parked my car. I started having an anxiety attack and went back inside the mall. I found a female mall security guard and told her what had happened. She was very nice and escorted me in a golf cart as we went all over the mall parking lot, searching for my vehicle.

I wasn't embarrassed to ask for help, but the most important thing for me was I needed to make sure that I was safe. I chose a person I could trust. At that moment when I was feeling lost and not trusting, it was a risk to select someone to confide in. I usually have a very good intuition, and each time I had a similar episode, I would also choose very trustworthy individuals to assist me during my disabling moments.

Nightmares

My most recurring nightmares were about when I was enlisted in the army and needed to receive my honorable discharge. Each time I was in this dream, I went to report to my duty station after everyone returned from the second tour in Iraq. I was in need of a new set of battle dress uniforms. I was the only one in formation wearing civilian clothes. I needed to search for my check-in allowance (uniform money) and also needed to purchase new physical training gear. Because of this, I got away with being out of uniform while every troop to my right or left were in full army uniform. I was waiting to get discharged, but my chain of command wouldn't release me. My leadership was somehow punishing me by not granting me my honorable discharge I worked so hard to obtain.

I was also waiting to get into the barracks, and for some reason, the entire post was empty. I saw a wall, but it kept me from going to the other side where my freedom was waiting for me. It took several tries before I was able to climb over this barrier that was keeping me captive. When I was on top of the wall ready to jump down to the other side to see what was waiting for me, I woke up, drenched in sweat. I had to change my pajamas for the second time that night.

Another repeating nightmare that would consume my soul was when my first sergeant would approach me and begin to yell in my face. After that, he would physically threaten me, and I had no one to advocate for me. Usually in the army when a soldier needs to go before his or her leadership, there is an advocate for the soldier.

I was frightened all over again just to be reminded about my first sergeant. It wasn't a particular first sergeant whom I dreamt about. I believe this was the result of all the first sergeants I had during my enlistment in the army. It included: my first sergeant in basic training, Advanced Individual Training (AIT); my duty station, Ft. Riley; and the one I was under in Kuwait for ODS Operation Desert Spring (ODS) in support of Operation Enduring Freedom (OEF).

But, the nightmare that scared me the most was the one about the man who sexually assaulted me while I was in the army. In this situation, I would fight him back and became his stalker and ended up about to hurt him. But then I would wake up, so I never saw myself damage my prey. Once I was awake, I couldn't go back to sleep right away because I was afraid of having another nightmare. I wanted to go back to sleep to see what would happen, but part of me didn't want to become a monster.

Enrolled and Dropped Classes

I went to a Maricopa Community College just as soon as I made Arizona my home state. I had enrolled in some classes in person and was ready to purchase my books. I made a visit to the financial aid office to ask about a book voucher. I accomplished this before at another Maricopa Community College, and I would always receive my book vouchers from that office.

When I went to the financial officer at this school, she was rude to me. She told me I couldn't get a book voucher there and just dismissed me. I was upset and confronted her about the way she had treated me. She didn't like what I said. I just walked away and told her I wasn't happy with the way the school had treated me. I went back in line to drop out of the classes I had just enrolled in for the semester.

She came out of her office and started to approach me. I told her to leave me alone, and I wasn't going to speak to her anymore. Then she began to walk behind me, and I told her to leave me alone and stop approaching me. She kept following me until I went to another room to calm down.

I told her that she had no right to treat me like this. I told her I had just came home from the war zone. I said their institution wasn't a good one because she was supposed to be there to help me, and she didn't. She only helped make matters worse for me.

As I was about to sit down and try to calm down, a security guard came by to see me but didn't approach me or say anything to me. I was still speaking to the lady and told her again to leave me alone so I could sit for a while and calm down. Once the security guard heard me say those words, he disappeared and so did the financial aid woman. When I was finished grounding myself, I left the campus.

Although there were people around me and saw what was going on, no one dared to look in my direction nor say anything to me. I noticed a couple who was there with their teenage son who looked as if he was fresh out of high school. *Well,* I thought to myself, *young man, welcome to the real world. You're not in high school anymore!*

It Wasn't Post Traumatic Stress Disorder

During the moment in my life when I had achieved success in grounding myself and gained emotional intelligence I decided to try the arts for more healing from PTSD. I enrolled at one of the Maricopa Community Colleges to receive a certificate in fashion design.

The first day of class everyone introduced themselves and shared why they chose the class or the fashion design program. I shared that I was an Iraqi War veteran who had been suffering from PTSD. I explained I had been searching for healing through the arts and discovered art is very therapeutic. I also added that I had been sewing since I was six years old and that fashion was my passion.

One day while I was in a clothing construction class, I got very sick. The instructor called the school emergency personnel team to have a look at me. After the team evaluated me, they called 911, and I was taken to the Phoenix V. A. Hospital, my hospital of choice. I was seen and then discharged after my diagnosis of chronic pain.

Later that week I was in another class where I had shared I was suffering from PTSD in the beginning of our semester. I got really sick again, but this time I couldn't speak because I was in too much pain. I couldn't advocate for myself because my back pain was at a level ten on a scale from one to ten. I felt like I was going to pass out at any moment.

The instructor called the school emergency team. They tried to evaluate me, but weren't successful. They called the first responders. When they arrived, the teacher yelled in front of the students, "She has that PTSD! She was in the Iraq War. I think she's having that PTSD moment right now!" The paramedics didn't clear the room. They immediately began to mistreat me. One of them made a fist and punched my chest. Then another one said that he wasn't going to pick me up. Instead, he pulled on me and threw me on the gurney. I yelled, "No! I don't want to go!" They strapped me down from head to feet. I couldn't move.

The paramedics wanted to know my name to record it in their documentation, but I refused to give it to them because they already knew who I was. They were the same paramedics who had helped me the same week when I was in the other classroom.

I asked them not to take me to the hospital across from the school because I wanted to go to the Phoenix V.A. Hospital, but they didn't honor my request.

When the paramedics dropped me off, they told the nurse I was 'Jane Doe' because I refused to give them my name, and that I had given them a hard time. I don't know what they had recorded on my medical chart, but I suspect they all had negative things to say. It all began at the college when the teacher yelled in front of the class that I was having a PTSD moment. The paramedics listened to her, which caused them to treat me the way that they did.

When I was finally in the emergency department, the nurse wasn't very kind. She asked me to tell her my name, and I refused. Then she sent an insurance representative to ask me some questions, but I also turned her down. After several tries, the lady left me alone.

When my assigned nurse found out about me being uncooperative, she came by with a team. First, she yanked my sweatshirt off, and said I was a threat to myself and to others around me.

Then she continued by taking off my prescription eyeglasses. After that, the staff group left. I grabbed my phone and called one of my brothers to come and get me because they had me there against my will. When they heard me, the nurse came and snatched my phone from my hand. I didn't try to fight her for it, but tried to keep her from retrieving it. She was pulling on it very violently and that hurt my wrist. I have arthritis and brittle bones, so I let her take it.

Five minutes later she came in with an entourage and handed me my phone and my school backpack the paramedics had transported with me. The hospital personnel had to inspect my bag to make sure I wasn't carrying anything that could be used as a weapon. I never said I was going to hurt myself or anyone. I have physical illnesses, too, that others didn't know about. Besides, it wasn't their business to know.

The hospital staff finally brought a tall Caucasian security guard to watch me, and he stood just outside my glass door. This was unbelievable to me. I had served my country, and been through so much in the process. Now, I was being mistreated by some ignorant and racist people. All of my abusers were the same skin color, I'm sorry to say. But I was in a Phoenix neighboring city where the demographic is not Latino or Hispanic residents and or workforce friendly. I hadn't experienced this type of racism since I was a child in California in the mid-1970's.

I needed to use the restroom, so I got up and began to march out of the room toward the restroom. The same nurse approached me and was in my personal space, but she stopped me. She asked me where I was going. I told her that I needed to use the restroom. She told me that I couldn't use the commode. She turned and pointed to the trash can in my room and told me to use the bathroom there. The room had glass walls, and it was visible to anyone in the area. I told her that I was not going to use the trash can as a toilet. I turned around to look at the security guard and told him to tell her she was violating my rights all over the place, she and everyone in the hospital. I said when I got out I was going to write a letter to Washington D.C., and it wasn't going to be pretty.

The guard signaled her to let me use the facilities. Finally, I was able to do my business. But it shouldn't have taken so much of a fight for me just to use the toilet. This was so wrong in so many ways. It reminded me of how some people of past decades must have felt when they had segregated restrooms.

After this incident, I grabbed my phone and called the local police department, telling them where I was and that I was there against my will. They sent out two police officers from the precinct to see me, one of whom was female. I explained to them how I had gotten sick at school and was transported to the hospital against my will. I told them the nurse and staff of the hospital had been mistreating me. I explained in detail all that had been done to me. The police officers then stepped out of the room, and I heard them speaking with the staff outside my room. Then I heard some laughter in the hallway. After that, the police came in the room and told me that I couldn't leave until someone came to pick me up. They left, and I just waited for my two brothers to come pick me up from that horrible place.

I kept my promise about writing a letter, but it wasn't going to be going to Washington D.C. I decided to write to my local Republican Senator who was always supporting me. I knew that I could count on him. In the letter I explained in detail everything that was done to me that day. I had the legal right to sue all of them, but I wasn't going to do that because I'm a woman of God and wanted this to be handled in a different manner.

I told him that I didn't want to gain any monetary compensation for any wrongdoing or for being discriminated against, but I didn't want them to get away with it either. I wanted them to get some extensive training. They needed to learn some valuable lessons. They should learn how to treat veterans with PTSD. They obviously had no idea that I wasn't under my PTSD moment when they were treating me. They just assumed it because someone said it, and the rest were treating me by what the chart said.

I sent copies of this letter to the mayor of the city, the president of the school district, the dean of the school, the head of the city's paramedics and to the patient advocate of the hospital. I wanted everyone in this city with power and authority to know how veterans were being treated and how they should be treated.

Declared Unemployable

My last attempt to become a professional in a career was when I wanted to became a kindergarten teacher. I was enrolled in a baccalaureate degree program at Rio Salado in Tempe. I majored in early childhood education and really enjoyed all of my classes. I couldn't continue because I got really ill and wasn't able to hold a job.

I had been injured in the army during basic training. I fell off of a truck that was parked, but because it was wet I slipped when I tried to climb in the back. I bumped my head on the top of the truck and then slipped and fell on the hitch part of the trailer. I landed on my bottom and hurt my tail bone.

I was no longer able to work, and Veteran's Affairs had declared me non-employable due to my many illnesses and my injury in the army. It took several months until I finally was declared unemployable and disabled.

I used this time to help myself get better and to find different ways to communicate with God and to know His character. I was proactive in my quest for mental and emotional healing.

Is anything bothering you? Has any misfortune occurred in your life? (You may use the next two pages to discuss something that is bothering you.)

How will you approach this situation?

Are you in need of some answers?

Where can you go to do research or speak to someone about getting information or some assistance?

King David went through some trials and tribulations and he petitioned to the Lord.

The Lord is my Shepherd, I lack nothing. He makes me lie down in green pastures, He leads me beside quiet water, He refreshes my soul. He guides me along the right paths for His name's sake. Even though I walk through the darkest valley, I will fear no evil, for you are with me; your rod and your staff, they comfort me. You prepare a table before me in the presence of my enemies. You anoint my head with oil; my cup overflows. Surely your goodness and love will follow me all the days of my life, and I will dwell in the house of the Lord forever.

Psalm 23:1-6 (NIV)

Goals

I still had to use up my Montgomery GI Bill. There were ten years remaining from my separation date to retrieve all of my educational benefits. I was not going to wait until the last minute to claim my funds for my higher ed learning. I immediately enrolled at Wayland Baptist University in the Biblical Studies program.

When I graduated from WBU with my bachelor' of science degree, my family came to my graduation. I was so happy to finally complete something I had started and worked hard to obtain. I was an individual who would begin something and then, after a while, would get bored or tired and abandon that goal or project. But this time, I was dedicated to finishing my educational endeavors.

The most important thing for me was that I was learning at a faith-based school that helped to learn more about God's character and love. This brought some healing into my life for this season.

Seminary School

Around 2011, I wanted to pursue a master's degree, and I decided to inquire about seminary school enrollment. After conducting my research, I found the university that met my educational needs. It was a very easy process, and the staff was wonderful in helping me with my enrollment to Fuller Theological Seminary. I started out with three courses but at the end of the first week, I dropped two of my classes. I stayed in my Church History course and completed the semester.

I was still dealing with PTSD and because I was still too sick, I didn't continue with my studies the following semester. I learned many things that I had often wondered about regarding Church History and the many crusades and the popes who were part of the Christian Roman Catholic Church history.

Fashion Design

It was now 2013, and I still had a desire to continue my education and use up the remaining funds of my GI Bill. I decided to attend fashion design school at Phoenix Community College. During the first day of class we were encouraged to introduce ourselves by the instructors. When it was my turn to speak I told the entire class that I was an Iraqi War Veteran and was experiencing PTSD. The reason that I chose the class was to heal from my diagnosis. I shared with the class that I was a right brained person and really enjoyed creating beautiful things. I continued to tell the class that I was exploring the arts to heal from my mental condition.

I was enrolled full time and planned to graduate with an associates of arts degree in Fashion Design. My favorite class was Fashion Design because I learned the history of fashion. I was also enrolled in basic garment construction. Although I already knew how to sew, it was a refresher course for me. Being in the class really helped me a lot because I was around other students who had the same interest as I did. They may have been a lot more ambitious than me, but at least we had art in common, and we all loved fashion and sewing.

I was enrolled in two Maricopa Community Colleges and I was getting real tired because the commute was getting to me. I had too much on my plate. In addition, I was also taking Hebrew courses through a Messianic Jewish place of worship. I ended up dropping some classes to be able to catch up with my fashion design courses. It was a difficult decision, and I decided to drop my Hebrew studies to make more time for my passion for fashion. The Hebrew classes weren't going to affect my grades because they weren't transferable ac-credited classes that would be added to any degree.

Learning about Deliverance

I enjoyed studying how to receive deliverance from various traumas that had God's people stuck in a dark place. I wanted to learn how to re-route the darkness and every negative action to the abyss where it be-longed. I had been doing some research on how to learn regarding this subject, and then I found a Christian woman who fights off ungodly spirits all the time. She is constantly in prayer and fighting these evil spirits that come in her path. I learned a lot about the subject of demons, but it wasn't enough at the time. I decided to not pursue disturbing that kingdom any longer at that time because I needed to get some deliverance accom-plished. I was still fighting demons myself, and I didn't want to step into a realm where I wasn't equipped for battle.

I found myself reading many books on prayer and deliverance because I wanted to search for a way to heal from my hurts. I knew I had been carrying a lot of events that took place in the war zone with me. It wasn't just the things that happened to me, but also things that happened to others and what they had witnessed.

I read a lot of Christian and faith-based books because my soul was mutilated, and I wanted to discover how I could get healed. I was searching for answers. Most of these books were self-help and the subjects ranged from prayer to deliverance.

Got Rid of the Soul Ties

I had learned that I needed to get rid of soul ties from a Christian Catholic woman who I met while I was working as a teacher's assistant at a Maricopa elementary school. I had past sexual assaults, and she told me that I needed to get rid of the soul ties that I had with each one of them. The men who had assaulted me had to leave my spirit woman. This was new to me, but it did make sense. Because it does say in the Bible when a man and woman have sexual intercourse that they become one. They are one in body and spirit.

God's Glory

I ordered a package of a program which included a compact disc and a workbook that was guaranteed to show me how to obtain God's glory. It really helped me to focus and go into the supernatural. I had some wells that were buried due to traumas in my life and what the teachings from this school did for me was to open up those wells that were a stumbling block for my kingdom living and striving to be all that God has created me to be.

The lesson that I had most interest in was when I learned new things about the Holy Spirit. This was something I needed. For years I have been able to speak in the heavenly language, but I still had so much more to learn and understand about the Holy Spirit. To understand Him as a person, not as commonly described by many as a gust of wind when He enters a room. The Holy Spirit is here among us because Jesus told His disciples that it would be done, receiving the Holy Spirit, once he left the earth to be with His Father in heaven.

He is with the spirit of Jesus, and He is with us. I always wondered about the Trinity, but once I finished studying this lesson it opened my spiritual lenses to a new dimension. I began seeing these beautiful iridescent type of lights that I hadn't seen since I was a toddler living in Mexico. I would often see these different shapes of beautiful iridescent figures flying around my house. They were so amazing that I have only seen those colors twice and that was when I was studying about God's Glory. The second time was a supernatural experience that I had in Italy in 2015. I write about it in the chapter titled Community Programs.

Becoming Holy for a Minute

While I was studying at home on God's glory, I continued to eat home-cooked meals and got up early every morning to run for two miles. Losing weight and eating healthy changed my entire body because I wasn't as depressed and anxious, plus it improved my spiritual life.

I woke up at 5 a.m. to read my Holy Bible first, then I prayed for about half an hour and, by the time it was 6 a.m., I was out the door running around the neighborhood.

At first I started walking for a mile. When my legs were strong enough, I walked for two miles. Then I began to jog for half a mile and walk the rest of the mile and a half. As my legs grew stronger, I began to run for one mile and then walk the other mile. I repeated this process until I could run the complete two miles.

I lost about thirty pounds and was feeling very healthy, physically and mentally. But I made a mistake in sharing with a sister that I was learning about God's glory and that I had been taking a course in the subject. This person discouraged me, and I left the ideas that I had learned in that study and also abandoned my healthy eating lifestyle. When I left my new pattern of life and went back to my old ways I began to fail at everything that I had worked so hard to achieve.

Christian Dance Camp

I was interested in attending a Messianic Jewish dance camp. I found one in Phoenix that was going to be held by a couple coming in from Nevada. I signed up online and proceeded with the registration. I arrived about half an hour late because I didn't know my way around that side of town.

I registered at the sign-in table and gave a donation, which is what was asked of those who wanted to participate. I went in and joined the dance crew. I was a bit nervous because I "have two left feet." I could hear the dance instructor telling her husband to lead me. I didn't mind because I was new at this, and I really enjoyed learning to dance unto the Lord.

When the event was over I introduced myself to the founder and owner of the dance camp. I shared with her that I was an Iraq War veteran who was exploring the arts to heal from PTSD. Then she gave me a word. She said that as I kept dancing unto the Lord that He was going to heal me of PTSD and use me to heal others. When I danced or praised unto the Lord that many were going to get their healing. Then she laid hands on me and prayed for me.

Messianic Jewish Dance Group

After meeting the dance camp lady, she recommended that I keep dancing and introduced a sister who held Messianic Dance meetings at her home in Chandler. Once we became connected, I attended her meetings on a regular basis for a couple of years. There were times we met at a Methodist Church in Tempe. When we had practiced enough several dances, we went out to nursing homes and other Messianic Jewish Churches and danced for the community.

My experience with the Messianic Jewish dancing was one of the most awesome things I have ever experienced in my life. Dancing unto the Lord brings me closer to Him. It makes me become more intimate with Him, and I get to know more about His character. I have also experienced more of His supernatural kingdom and mysteries that I even can't decipher.

What is a short-term goal, one month to six months, you have in mind? (Use the remaining page to answer the question)

Follow up on your short-term goal.

Scriptures for personal growth and development.

When I was a child, I talked like a child, I thought like a child, I reasoned like a child. When I became a man, I put the ways of childhood behind me.

I Corinthians 13:11 (NIV)

I keep asking that the God of our Lord Jesus Christ, the Glorious Father, may give you the Spirit of wisdom and revelation, so that you may know him better. I pray that the eyes of your heart may be enlightened in order that you may know the hope to which he has called you, the riches of his glorious inheritance in his holy people.

Ephesians1 17-18: (NIV)

And this is my prayer that your love may abound more and more in knowledge and in depth of insight.

Philippians 1:9 (NIV)

Do not...their unspiritual mind. They have lost connection with the head, from whom the whole body, supported and held together by its ligaments and its sinews, grows as God causes it to grow.

Colossians 2:18-19 (NIV)

The Fifth Floor

The first time I experienced feeling like my world was ending was one afternoon when I was driving around El Mirage, Arizona. I felt a sense of disconnection to the world and found myself in a horrible place. I was driving and got lost. I didn't know which direction to turn to make it home safely, and to make matters worse, I was very troubled in my mind.

I looked at my surroundings and couldn't remember where I was. It was a horrific time for me because I began to have an anxiety attack. When I realized I needed help getting back home, I called my brother and told him what was going on. I waited patiently in my car for my brother as I remained parked on the side of the road.

He arrived, and I managed to follow him home. I wasn't as scared anymore because I knew I was being assisted by someone I knew and trusted. About ten minutes later, we were finally home.

I entered the house, went directly to my room and decided that I needed to rest. My body was exhausted because I had been so anxious that I got really ill and didn't remember where I was. I remember I felt like I was not in my body. My physical body was present, but my mind and soul seemed like they were not available. I had checked out for quite a while and lost track of time during this episode. I was experiencing something new, and I was afraid to face whatever it was. I can give it a name, it was PTSD, and it made me feel like I was in another place; somewhat like a dream, but with a lot of fear. This wasn't a good feeling at all. It simulated a nightmare without an ending.

This was definitely the beginning stages of my PTSD moments, and I was not prepared for what was going to happen in the next ten years. I learned how to deal with my fears through trial and error.

In general, I can describe PTSD as a conglomerate of various emotions, feelings, memories, triggers and actions, all packed into one. Yet if one is looking to dissect this condition, I would say that it's very difficult to describe because every service member and or veteran experiences PTSD differently.

The First Dangerous Trigger (2008)

I dismissed what happened to me the following day when I woke up. I wasn't in the same spirit as the previous day. For some reason, I still noticed I was wondering if I was better or if my mind was playing a trick on me. I had an unsettling feeling that wouldn't go away. The next day I went to visit my mother at her apartment in Phoenix. I was fine while I was staying with her. I don't know what triggered me, but without any warning, I was back in Iraq. I was stuck there and was voicing events that took place while I was deployed to Baghdad.

My mother approached me and asked me if I was all right. I couldn't answer her. I was in Iraq, and I couldn't leave my post. I saw myself during one of my guard duty assignments when I was up in a tower alone.

My mother called 911 and the Phoenix paramedics arrived on scene. One firefighter wanted to take my vitals, but I wouldn't let him because I didn't want him to touch me. I remember telling the paramedics that I didn't want them to touch me. Some minutes were lost for me after that because the next thing I remember were two women from Phoenix Crisis Intervention coming to speak with me.

Before I knew it, one of them was asking me questions and went with me to Baghdad, where I was mentally and emotionally. I described to her what I saw and everything related to the scenery. I told her I was cold and scared because it was dark up there. I was alone and afraid we would get mortared, and I would die up on the tower.

This young lady was a professional and gently took me out of the war zone and helped ground me enough to consent to be transported to the Phoenix V.A. Hospital, so I could admit myself to the psychiatric ward.

When I arrived at the emergency department I had to be chaperoned. My personal belongings were taken from me and placed in a plastic bag and stored somewhere until the day of my discharge. I was finally admitted to the fifth floor of the hospital. I went into my room. I was there alone without a roommate and that was awesome to me because I didn't want to have to share a room with another female. For the moment, I was the only female in the psychiatric ward. There was another ward for those who needed more help, and I was blessed because I didn't need to be there.

The staff gave me my medication prescribed to me by my medical doctor. I was now in a place where I felt safe and didn't have to worry about anything other than getting my mental health back to the point I could be released from being a patient of the fifth floor.

As a patient of the psychiatric ward, there were rules to follow and it was recommended that we attend the classes that were available to us. Each day there was something different to do, and that included classes on mental health.

My favorite moment during my stay on the fifth floor was we had a counselor who came to visit us, and she played her guitar and sang songs with us. She sang a couple of country songs and some "oldies but goodies". I joined in with the rest of the patients, and we had a good time singing all of the songs.

I met many wonderful people while I sought help at the psychiatric ward in the Phoenix V.A. Hospital. There was a patient who was an elderly man, and I noticed how lonely he was. He didn't have any luck with his family, and from what I heard, they weren't too happy with him. He feared that they would want to admit him permanently to the psychiatric hospital. I felt sad for him because I put myself in his shoes and imagined my family wanting to get rid of me like that. That was a sad moment to witness. I was grieved because I couldn't do anything to help him.

I wanted to vacate this place when I was ready. I wasn't trying to get out right away, but at the same time, I wasn't trying to stay longer than needed. I made sure that I attended the classes we were scheduled for each day. After about a week, my doctor authorized my discharge. The only thing I didn't like about this visit was that an intern psychologist misdiagnosed me as bipolar, gave me medication for this condition, and then dismissed me from the psychiatric ward.

The Next Admittance to the Psychiatric Ward

It was now 2010, and I was depressed because something triggered me and aggravated my PTSD. This time, I had a plan. I was going to get drunk and stab myself to death. It was the Fourth of July weekend and it also was evident that I needed professional help. I battled back and forth in my mind. *Should I do this or should I wait to see when I will get better?*

I was hurting inside, and I didn't know how to receive my healing. I needed to let go of all that was hurting me, but I had no idea how to even begin.

I made the decision to just get help instead of committing suicide. I called a friend and told her that I was going to admit myself to the Phoenix V.A. Hospital because I was suicidal, and she said that she wanted to go with me to see me check in. I asked my sister, who was my designated driver to the hospital, if my friend Lisa would be able to ride with us to the hospital. I asked her to please give her a ride home after I was checked in the emergency department for the fifth floor.

This time I was thinking about hurting myself, and it wasn't a good feeling. I knew that I needed help, but didn't know who to turn to here on earth. During this time, I felt the deep wounds in my spirit and soul. I didn't know how to receive my spiritual healing. I was just going in circles and didn't know how to escape.

As soon as I was admitted to the fifth floor, I was given my hospital gowns and hygiene products to use during my stay. Then I was escorted to my room.

I was so depressed that my mind was all foggy, and I couldn't think clearly. Yet, at the same time, it was like there was a lot of garbage in my mind. The garbage needed to be cleansed out, but I didn't know how to begin the process. I desperately needed professional help.

A typical day in the ward would consist of waking up, and then going to pick up our medication at the nurses' station. This took a couple of minutes prior to receiving our meals. After breakfast if there was time, we could take a shower before our first activity. These lessons were not mandatory, but if it showed on your medical chart and record that you were attending the various groups and counseling sessions, it would help get you on the discharge list. All of these programs we participated in helped to speed up the process of receiving our discharge. The longer patients took on being part of the community, the longer they would remain on the fifth floor.

After we were finished with the classes, we had free time to watch t.v. in the dayroom. We had a selection of activities in the dayroom besides t.v. There was quite a lot of puzzles to choose from, and plenty of board games, such as checkers and chess. Also during our free time, we could make phone calls using the designated phone in the hallway.

I eventually got a roommate, and she was very cooperative with me. I didn't have any problems with her at all. We knew each other's boundaries and never crossed any lines. It also helped that she was much older than me. She must have been in her mid-60's.

I noticed something that wasn't right about her behavior. She paid too much attention to the fact that I was thin, and she wanted to lose weight. She began to skip her meals. She would take the trays of food, but not eat and just starve herself. I made the decision to let someone in authority know about her behavior and from that moment on she was watched to make sure that she ate all of her food.

When I was there this time, things were a bit different for me because I got special treatment when it came to my food choice. One day I asked for a salad and was prepared the most nutritious salad that I have ever seen. There was so much green on that plate I was enjoying the attention that I was getting. A male patient asked how I managed to get what I wanted. I just looked at him and smiled and thought about God.

Finally, I had been there for about a week and was ready to go back home to my daily routine. Which was basically surviving, attending my doctor's visits at the Phoenix V.A. Hospital and sleeping most of the day. During this period in my life I was very depressed and was so sleepy during the day I often took several naps. I wasn't in school and didn't have any future goals to achieve at this moment. I was just existing because I didn't know how to live anymore. I was so lost in my head and heart that I didn't know if I was coming or going.

The Next Visit the Psych Ward

The next time I had to admit myself at the emergency department for psychiatric help was in 2015. I had been very active in church ministries, but I was still hurting from the sexual assault I experienced during my service in the army. I went into a deep depression and was suicidal once again.

I would share my testimony about being hurt to others, and I would receive negative feedback. Most people would discourage me from speaking about it and suggest I was always going to keep getting hurt if I continued talking about it. The reason why I would speak about what happened to me was so people would understand that I had been deeply hurt, and I needed to be around people who were going to keep me safe. But after some time, I realized I needed to be delivered and began to pray to the Lord, so that He would show me what I needed to do to get my healing.

One day while I was working at a school district in Phoenix as a teacher's assistant, I met a lady who worked with a special needs children. She shared with me that she had a deliverance ministry when she was younger.

During our conversation, she taught me that I needed to free myself from all those spirits that had been attached to me from all my sexual assaults. She made sense, and I followed the instructions she gave me. In a sense she taught me how to get rid of the soul ties connection from a past or present individual(s). (This is similar to what I mentioned in the chapter entitled *Goals* regarding the release of soul ties).

I made a list of all the names of those who attacked me and those men who had been casual acquaintances in my life. It was important to purge out any and all memories I had of all the men I had any encounters with who had any soul ties. Then I prayed to the Lord that I be released from bondage of the soul ties to each name that I mentioned to God. Then I felt a deliverance. I was still missing something, but I didn't know what just yet.

Here I Go Again (2017)

It would be another two years before I would admit myself again to the Phoenix V.A. Hospital's emergency department for suicidal ideation. It was now 2017, and I had accomplished many good things in life. I was still suffering from my past hurts. Then something un-expected occurred. There was a fire in my apartment complex, and I had to vacate the premises. The Phoenix Fire Department arrived on the scene and put the fire out. No one was hurt, and that was a good thing. But since some damage was done in one of the apart-ments above mine, we were told to move out because the smoke damaged the rest of the apartments in that building. Some of the tenant's property was damaged by the water the firemen released to put out the fire.

This was very scary for me because I couldn't sleep in my apartment anymore. I had to find somewhere to spend the night. The next day, I had to start finding somewhere else to live. I went to stay with my mom while I waited to be accepted as a resident at a local women veteran's low-income housing complex.

This situation disrupted my life and brought stress upon me to the point I became afraid of becoming homeless once again. Soon I became depressed. I had somewhere to live for the time being, but it wasn't the same life I had before. This time around I was renting a room from someone, and I wasn't used to that. I wasn't free to do things as I was used to like coming and going without telling anyone one of my whereabouts. This new living arrangement just disrupted my life. I became deeply depressed because I felt like I was someone who was down on her luck. In a sense, I was homeless. I was fortunate to find that local veteran women's low-income housing unit where I applied to be a resident. The process took about three weeks before I was accepted and moved in. But I was still depressed and suicidal. At this point in my life I realized my spirit and soul needed to heal at the same time, once and for all. I needed a divine intervention for that to occur. But in the meantime, I still wanted to end my life. I needed immediate help.

I decided to turn myself into the Phoenix V.A. Hospital. I went in for a routine appointment and expressed to a vocational counselor that I was thinking about hurting myself. She asked me how I was going to accomplish that, and I told her that I was going to do whatever popped in my head. She kept me there in her office until another staff member came by to take me to the Mental Clinic.

Once I was checked into the clinic, I was assigned a chaperone to make sure I wasn't going to hurt myself. Then my psychiatrist wanted to see me briefly before I was sent to the emergency department because she had a student with her who wanted to see me to learn from my story. I was cooperative because I was asked if I authorized him to be there and observe me.

When I arrived at the emergency department, I was placed in a room with a surveillance camera. There was an extra pair of eyes watching me that day. But I didn't mind because it was for my safety.

There weren't any female rooms available at that time. The V.A. Hospital was authorized to send me to an outside facility where I would be receiving my medical treatment. A call was made to an ambulance company to transport me to the nearest psychiatric clinic with which they worked. Arrangements were made for me to be transferred. When I arrived at this new place, I was asked to sit and wait in a room for several minutes. After that I was given a hospital gown and slippers to change into. I had to turn in all my possessions to them for safe keeping until I was discharged.

This time was different for me because after I felt better and was on my psychiatric medication, the doctor released me to go home. Before I was discharged, I was asked if I wanted to participate in a weekly group counseling session available there at the clinic. I accepted the offer because I wanted to heal and have a healthy mind.

I was discharged and sent home in an Uber taxi. The hospital paid for my ride home, which was quite a commute since this place was located nearly twenty miles southwest of Phoenix.

Do you get triggers?

Where can you go or what can you do when this happens?

If you are not feeling well and or are experiencing suicidal thoughts, please pick up the phone and dial 911. You may find a suicide hotline on the internet and write the number here.

____

Scriptures to read for anxiety and fear.

> *Be anxious for nothing, but in everything in prayer and supplication in prayer with thanksgiving let your request be made known to God.*
>
> Philippians 4:6 (NIV)

> *For God has not given us a spirit of fear, but of power and of love and of a sound mind*
>
> 2 Timothy 1:7 (NIV)

> *Take my yoke upon you and learn from me, for I'm humble and gentle at heart, and you will find rest in your souls.*
>
> Matthew 11:29 (NIV)

My Love for Him

I have to give God all the credit for my surviving and thriving with PTSD. Although I have had so many people who entered my life to help me heal, I must give Him honor where honor is due. His great love for me and His taking care of me has been evident to me throughout my entire life. He has shown me over and over again that He loves me and, in return, I must love Him with all my heart, mind, sprit and soul.

Jesus replied, "Love the Lord your God with all your heart and with all your soul and with all your mind."

Matthew 22:37 (NIV)

I enjoyed going on dates with Jesus on numerous occasions. When I selected the place to have lunch with Him, I would bring my Bible and notebook along with me and have lunch at a restaurant. After I ordered my food, I opened my Bible and searched for scriptures to read. Then I would write messages in my notebook related to God's love for me.

My favorite book to read is Psalms because it helps the reader to understand what he or she is feeling. I would take my time eating and writing, and when I was finished, I gave the waitress a $20 tip. I did this because I took my time at the table. I knew that she would have normally waited on at least three different customers in the booth I was occupying. That's how long I would take on my date with Jesus; that's how much He matters to me. He is number one in my life!

I also love the Holy Spirit, and one day I learned to make time for Him. I read more about the Holy Spirit from the Holy Bible, and it really changed my life. This was the beginning stages of some of my healing from various medical conditions like insomnia, severe back pain and hypervigilance.

When I first dedicated time for the Holy Spirit was when I lived in El Mirage with my youngest brother. This was the first time I spent many hours with the Holy Spirit. I just remember feeling real grounded and peaceful when I acknowledged Him and asked Him to please visit with me. I began to have a normal conversation with Him just like I would with a human being here on earth. Soon I began to feel a soft touch on my forehead and then it became a soothing touch. Before I knew it, I was down on the floor in the prone position, face down with an unmovable body. It's such a supernatural experience that it leaves me so relaxed that I feel like I'm on some type of high.

When I date the Holy Spirit, I always visit with Him inside the four walls of my residence because I don't know what will happen. He might have me fall down without any warning. I don't want to scare anyone or have someone call the authorities on me for disturbing the peace because anything can happen when I allow the Holy Spirit to take over me.

When I'm under the guidance of the Spirit I can be a bit loud and extremely bold. The moment begins in my belly and then rushes to excite my soul as my spirit begins to rejoice. After that occurs, I'm so deep in God's love that nothing else matters to me. I lose track of time as I enter into His holy presence.

As ambassadors of Jesus Christ, we have the freedom to rejoice in Him. Being in the presence of the Holy Spirit is so far the most powerful experience that I have ever known!

At that time Jesus, full of joy through the Holy Spirit, said, "I praise you Father, Lord of heaven and earth because you have hidden those things from the wise and learned, and revealed them to little children. Yes, father for this was your pleasure."

Luke 10:21 (NIV)

I have loved him individually and corporately. During each moment it varies. Each time it's a different experience for me because I welcome the Holy Spirit to take over to shift the atmosphere.

When I'm loving Him individually, for example, it's the occasion when I set aside a time for prayer and speak to Him about my needs, the needs of those whom I know, as well as the intercession for those who are hurting. I must have the discipline to search for Him individually and freely know Him at a more intimate level.

An example of loving God corporately could be during church service when the worship team is leading the congregation in songs of worship. We gather together with our brothers and sisters to welcome the Holy Spirit to shift the atmosphere and allow Him to take over the service and speak to our hearts. When this takes place, healing will follow along with God's peace.

Love for Others

"A new command I give you: love one another. As I have loved you, so you must love one another. By this everyone will know that you're my disciples. If you love one another."

John 13:34 (NIV)

"If you love those who love you, what reward will you get? Are not even tax collectors doing that? And if you greet you're your own people, what are you doing more than others? Do not even pagans do that? Be perfect, therefore, as your heavenly Father is perfect.

Matthew5:46-48 (NIV)

There was a brother in the church whom I loved, and I wrote a poem for him for his celebration service. He passed away April 15, 2017, just after his birthday.

I was inspired to write about how I had felt about him for all the years that I knew him as a brother in the Lord.

The Wonderful Things

As I sit here and ponder I feel nostalgic about some of the wonderful things that in God's Kingdom I knew you were.

I will always remember you as the anointed
musician
That helped me to know more about God's
character.

Each time that I drove my car onto the church
parking lot
my heartbeat rushed and shifted to a higher level.
Because my entire DNA anticipated hearing
the warring beat that aggressively exiled the devil.

I enjoyed listening to the supernatural pulse that
lit up my world like a wildfire, thus your spirit I
will miss.
God gave you authority, power and an angelic
language
on the congas to rescue my soul out of the Abyss.

My ears heard your artistic ways with numerous melodies which warmed and made my heart
smile.
They conquered all the storms that were in my
life,
even the tiniest sin to every fear that was vile.

My thoughts and body felt safe at the sound of the ancient drums
that awakened and fortified all the five waves that wire my brain.
These brain waves are the Alpha, Beta, Theta, Delta and Gamma.
The Theta always connects me to God's mysteries, and I feel no pain.

You also owned the ministry of deliverance. You rescued me from
that grotesque beast of the war that I brought home, called PTSD
I always delighted in dancing to the tamed pulse of your percussion.
The first time that I shimmied down the church aisle, it set me free!

Minister of the Gospel through you I learned to love in a new way.
There are many types of love, in our Godly life there's one that matters. This agape love is never to be taken lightly because it covers over all the sins from hate to murder, even unnecessary chatters.

I proclaim to the atmosphere that for you I carried healthy love,
because God said to me, "I love and want him, what do you say?"
I replied, "He's yours my Abba. I shall fearlessly love you the most
because in your kingdom and presence, my Lord, I want to stay.

There were so many hidden things that remained in my heart.
I wanted to convey all of them to you when you passed me by.
Today I unleash to you and all ears that can hear that you,
Dear man of God you meant a lot to me. You were not just any guy!

You impacted my life in so many precious ways that I lost count.
Today I'm victorious, innocent like a dove and as shrewd as a snake.
You must take ear to the fact that we all meet people in our lives
and know that the Lord planned our steps. He didn't make a mistake.

You were a musician, minister, healer, man of God and much more.
You praised and worshipped the Lord. He has called you, "friend."
Salvation, grace and mercy He has offered to you for free.
I loved you beyond words that you could ever comprehend!

Loving my Parents (is also loving God)

This next poem reminds me of how beautiful my life was during my age of innocence (two to three years old) when I lived in Ensenada, Baja California, Mexico, with my maternal grandparents.

The Vineyards

Something occurred between my parents that caused my grandparents to become my temporary guardians, when I was a toddler.
They lived in Ensenada, Baja California, Mexico.
One day my grandpa took me to the vineyard where he worked as the main farmer.

My eyes grew big at the sight of the grapes. Grandpa spoke to me, "My daughter, select and eat as many grapes as your little heart desires."Stay here, don't move, because I must go off for a tiny moment to make sure I work the hours that this job requires.".

I was too young to understand those grown up things. Then one sad day mother and father came for me, and now I was living with them.

My small three-year-old mind just didn't know what happened behind closed doors. My innocent thoughts didn't comprehend.

Father moved us to a property that had a beautiful adobe house, outhouse and an enormous back yard where I could roam free.

One day I was given some wonderful news. Mother came home with a baby. I had a brother and now we were a family of three.

Life was wonderful. I enjoyed running in our backyard, chasing dragonflies and hiding in the tall grass with my little brother.

I experienced separation again, my father left for the United States leaving me, my sibling and pregnant mother.

I mustered energy to accept that our family was growing at a steady
speed, making me a big sister just one more time.

Little did I know that I would be relocating to the other side, and it wasn't going to cost me a single dime.

We were being transported to the new land with a different approach than the traditional crossing over the fence.

My family was soon to be together in America by traveling through the border. This trip had me in suspense.

I missed my father so much and hoped that he would return but that was not in his plans. He sent for us first, then mother was next.

I wasn't frightened being alone with a Navajo lady who was family by marriage, although I didn't know what to expect.

We waited at the bus station in Mexicali and then boarded with our aunt who spoke a language that was foreign to us.

Mother told us to pretend to understand every word that she spoke as we traveled to Long Beach, California, on the bus.

She opened her mouth and spoke many words to me and my siblings. It was strange to me to have to fake to be fluent in her tongue.

I looked at it like it was a game as I naively submitted to my elders who assigned me to a task to make sure things didn't go wrong.

All I could think in my five-year-old brain was to be reunited with our father who employed someoneto transport our beautiful mother.

She would be joining us soon, so we met up with our family that lived in Long Beach. Finally she arrived, and we were all together.

I still visit the vineyards when I'm feeling nostalgic and, full of dreams, plans, goals and a healthy spiritual life of success.

My mind reminisces with that three-year-old little girl that once roamed the vineyards in Baja California, a life I desperately miss!

I fell in love with everything that was associated with the U.S Army

The U.S. Army Values

Loyalty

Bear true faith and allegiance in the US Constitution, the Army, and other soldiers.
Be loyal to the nation and its heritage.

Duty

Fulfill your obligations.

Accept responsibility for your own actions and those entrusted to your care.

Find opportunities to improve oneself for the good of the group.

Respect

Rely upon the golden rule.

How we consider others reflects upon each of us, both personally and as professional organization.

Selfless Service

Put the welfare of the nation, the Army, and our subordinates before your own.

Selfless service leads to organizational teamwork and encompasses discipline, self-control and faith in the system.

Honor

Live up to all the Army values.

Do what is right, legally and morally.

Be willing to do what is right even when no one is looking.

It is our "moral compass" and inner voice.

Courage

Our ability to face fear, danger, or adversity, both physical and moral courage.

The Soldier's Creed

I am an American soldier
I am a warrior and a member of the team
And live the army values
I will always place the mission first
I will never accept defeat
I will never quit
I will never leave a fallen comrade
I am disciplined physically and mentally tough
Trained and proficient in my warrior tasks and
    drills
I always maintain my arms, my equipment and
    myself
I am an expert and I am a professional
I stand ready to deploy, engage and destroy
    enemies

Of the United States of America in close combat
I am a guardian of freedom and the American
way of life
I am an American Soldier

I also loved my weapon that was assigned to me. The following is:

The Rifleman's Creed

This is my rifle. There are many like it, but this one is mine. It is my life. I must master it as I must master my life. Without me my rifle is useless. Without my rifle, I am useless. I must fire my rifle true. I must shoot him before he shoots me. I will... My rifle and I know that what counts in war are not the round we fire, the noise of our burst, or the smoke we make. We know that it is the hits that count. We will hit.

My rifle is human, even as I am human, because it is my life. Thus, I will learn it as a brother. I will learn its weaknesses, its strengths, its parts, its accessories, its sights and its barrel. I will keep my rifle clean and ready even as I am clean and ready. We will become part of each other.

Before God I swear this creed. My rifle and I are the defender of my country. We are the masters of our enemy.

Loving Relatives Past and Present

I was in the mood for love during my recovery time from PTSD. I fell in love with the fact that I have ancestors who were successful in the community. I realized I was carrying the same blood, the same genes and, if they could achieve greatness, so could I. That helped me to get out of my depression mode and encouraged me to stop feeling sorry for myself.

I remembered that my great-grandfather from my father's side of the family had founded a town in Mexicali, Baja California, Mexico, and he employed several hundred employees. My great-aunt from my mother's side was the co-founder of the same town as my great-grandfather. I come from businessmen and women, and that's something to be proud of all the days of my life.

I also have strong women in my bloodline. For example, some of the women from the 1940's era who became widows with children, they wouldn't remarry and worked hard to make sure their children had all the provisions they needed.

Adding to the wonderful list of relatives I have, there are also medical doctors, lawyers, schoolteachers, nurses, bankers, excellent blue-collar workers, and homemakers in my generation.

Time for a Self-Evaluation

I knew that, after realizing I come from such great people, that I have it in me to succeed. I decided to take the victim mentality out of my mind. There came a moment in my life when I had to motivate myself and encourage myself to become something great. To do this I would have to reflect on past successes in order to build myself up and inspire myself to begin dreaming again. I searched in my head one by one my past victories, both small and large, and rated them.

It was great to see those positive things written on a piece of paper because I could visualize some things that were real I had accomplished. Then, I motivated myself to believe in myself again and to dream again. To do this, I needed to get rid of some characteristics that were stumbling blocks and had me in a stuck mode.

I decided to get rid of behaviors that were getting me nowhere like gossiping, complaining, bitterness and fear to name a few. I had to do an inventory of my character. When I was finished, I filled my entire being with positive traits likes the ones in the army values so that I would be whole. The purpose of purging the negative is to replace it with positive characteristics so I won't be left empty.

My Culture

I fell in love with who I am as far as culture is concerned. I decided to so some research one day on the origin of my last name and discovered it's found in the Belarus Jewish database. I made the decision to connect with a Messianic Jewish Church to be familiar with the Jewish culture. It was a possibility that I had some ties to the Hebrew culture although I hadn't performed any DNA testing. I was going by what the Belarus Jewish database was telling me. It was amazing that the spelling of my last name varied, depending upon the nation and the language to which they were exiled.

I associated with a Jewish Messianic Temple in Phoenix. I was still attending my home church at V.O. East Phoenix and was serving in my assigned ministries. I couldn't quit what I had started, but I couldn't turn down the opportunity to find out more about my identity.

Learning from this new community helped me to appreciate Jesus and the gospel even more. This experience also brought me closer to the Holy Spirit. I learned more about God's character, and in addition, I became more fearful of God.

One of my favorite things about the Messianic movement is the blowing of the shofar, the trumpet. In the Holy Bible it speaks about it so many times. This experience also helped me with my healing process of PTSD. The hearing and listening of this instrument set the captives free. Deliverance takes place! For several weeks at a time during one year I searched the internet for shofar blowing and played the music for about twenty minutes, allowing my spirit to soak in the sound of the shofar. The musical vibrations soothed my soul and grounded my entire being. It was an excellent spiritual awakening and very educational at the same time. I was so blessed to be able to learn so much from this community.

Loving Nature

One day I made a trip to Payson, Arizona, with a friend and brought a picnic basket and a writing tablet and pen with me to practice some of my writing skills. It was my intention to start writing as soon as I arrived at our destination. But it didn't occur that way. The Lord spoke to my heart and said to me, "Look at the scenery;

just admire it." I began to look around and to appreciate what I saw and thanked God for His wonderful creation. Then I envisioned Him creating the earth and everything that breaths and lives from the plants, animals and mankind.

I also appreciated the weather was always much cooler in Payson, and during the summer it was an excellent place to escape the Phoenix heat. It was definitely a plus to leave the city behind for a day and enjoy a quiet day with nature far away from all the city noise.

I found it very therapeutic to be around the many green plants and trees nature has to offer. This is something I had been needing for a long time. But, because I had a fear to travel long distances to places I've never been before, I didn't challenge myself. This change was only possible when I began to love God all over again and appreciate everything that He had done for me. This also included my gratitude for all the things He has created. I combined my love for nature with my love for writing. This combination helped me to enjoy writing and encouraged me to write my first book, *From Baja to Baghdad and Back to the Barracks.* And I didn't stop there. I went on to write and publish my second book based on my domestic violence story, *Chasing Dragonflies.*

I encourage you to fall in love or love two things all over again. (you may use the remaining page to write about what you love or want to love again)

Scriptures on love.

For God so loved the world that he gave his one and only Son, that whoever believes in him shall not perish but have eternal life.

John 3:16 (NIV)

The second is this, Love your neighbor as yourself. There is no commandment greater than this.

Mark 12:31 (NIV)

A new command I give to you to love one another. As I have loved you. By this everyone will know that you are my disciples. If you love one another.

John 13:34-35 (NIV)

And now these three remain: faith, hope and love. But the greatest of these is love.

1 Corinthians 13:13 (NIV)

Thank you Lord for loving us so much that you gave your only begotten Son to die on the cross for our sins. It is your love that covers over a multitude of sins.

I Peter 4:8 (NIV)

Community Programs

When I enrolled at the Phoenix Veteran's Affairs Hospital in 2005, there weren't many programs available to assist female veterans who had just returned to the states from the war zone. For this reason, I was sent to the Phoenix Veteran's Center to see a counselor. I didn't connect with this counselor and, within the first month of seeing her, I abandoned my visits with her.

I took PTSD 101 at the Phoenix V.A .Hospital, and during the lecture one of the counselors who was speaking told us he had done research on wars. He found out PTSD had been around since the times of Homer, but it was called something different. Upon learning this I did my own research as soon as I got home and went into prayer. I searched Biblical history, PTSD and what surprisingly came to my mind was King David.

I realized that King David was a warrior about seven times over and most likely suffered from PTSD. It is no coincidence that he wrote the book of Psalm.

He sinned with Bathsheba at a time when all kings go to war, but he stayed home. Why did he stay home? Could it be that he was battling depression or some type of war syndrome?

This made me aware that my spirit needed to be healed. What I needed was Jesus and a lot of help from the church. I began to search for help from so many organizations and was wondering how being part of a church community was going to help me heal from PTSD.

New Counselor

It would be another three years before I made another attempt at searching for a counselor, and this time it was at the Phoenix V.A. Hospital. I was assigned a female counselor who was an expert in MST (Military Sexual Trauma). I had weekly visits with her, and then she asked if I wanted to participate in a group she facilitated for women diagnosed with PTSD. We could share during group as much or as little as we wanted to say about ourselves. I felt safe within the group session the first day and did share a bit about my traumas and was challenged to open up a bit. I attended the group and individual counseling for a couple of years until my counselor said something to me that was unacceptable, and I fired her.

My next counselor, Carol, was at the Phoenix Veteran's Center and I was pleased with her because I connected with her and spoke about my faith with her. This was something that my previous counselor didn't and couldn't understand about me. That had kept me stuck for several years.

Carol was overseeing a veteran women's PTSD group and invited me to be a part of it. This group helped out a lot because, as a participant, we were given the opportunity to speak about what had happened to us during our enlistment. For many women veterans this was the first time speaking about sexual assault experiences, which are very difficult to speak about. We all were very patient with the women as they shared, and we also had a lot of compassion for each other. We reminded each other that we were not alone.

During the meeting of this group I met a veteran lady, Betty, who had been a devout Catholic after her separation from the military. She knew about a Franciscan Roman Catholic Church in Arizona that had a veteran's ministry. This church operated retreats to help veterans heal from PTSD. Betty told me she was going to give me a flier about the next retreat, so that I could contact someone about becoming a participant.

I wasn't exactly sure what the retreat was about, but Betty briefed me on it and told me that it would help heal my broken spirit. That's exactly what I was searching for.

Unfortunately, I didn't receive that in my home church because I was searching for someone who had been in the war zone who also was a believer; someone I could relate to.

Through the Franciscan order, I found out about St. Francis. St. Francis had been a warrior and a prisoner of war. He knew most likely what it was like to have post-traumatic stress. St. Francis was from a family of merchants. His father was a fabric merchant and wanted Francis to join him in his business after he finished serving in the military. But Francis turned all that down because he wanted to do something different. He didn't care about status in society. He was looking for something greater than what the world had to offer.

More Healing

In December, 2015, was my first experience with a program that was secular and spiritual at the same time. This program helped to ground me spiritually, and soon after I began to use my voice.

I almost got to assist my sister in the Lord at a revival on a Native American reservation, and I decided to cancel on her to attend this retreat for veterans because I was in need of this group. I decided that I wasn't going with her because I had already made a commitment to attend the retreat. I didn't promise her that I would be going to her event. I actually said that I might go, which she took it as a definite yes.

I was told that one could share as little or as much as he or she wanted. We were encouraged to speak about our faith. This was something I had been longing for, and this retreat came at the right time.

The retreat started in the afternoon. After everyone checked in, each participant went to his or her assigned room to unpack and wait around until dinner time at 6 p.m. The first session began after dinner in the chapel. That's when I arrived, right in the middle of the session when I heard a young female veteran speaking to the group. They were all sitting in chairs and had formed a large circle. She was speaking about why she was participating in the retreat. She had experienced posttraumatic stress after the Gulf War and wanted to receive healing and became interested when someone recommended this retreat to her.

She was the last one to introduce herself to the group when I arrived. Since I arrived in time to tell my peers some information about myself, I was excited to share a slice of my story with my new friends.

In the next exercise we were encouraged to speak with the person to our right and find out as much information about him or her to share with the group. Once we were finished, we spoke a little bit about our new friend to the entire community of veterans. This was the beginning of the retreat. Once this assignment was complete, we wrapped it up and went to our rooms.

On Saturday there were several exercises and assignments that we completed. The first one was to select some crayons, markers and colored pencils and a large sheet of paper, the size of a poster. We were instructed to draw a story representing our life. Then we could discuss our story board. It was my turn, and I shared with three other veterans and a civilian, two of whom were male and the other was female. The facilitator was not a veteran. The female and one of the male veterans were both Gulf War veterans, so I could relate to them about PTSD.

When I heard their stories it was like I was listening to part of my testimony. They had experienced some of the same things I had and that created a special bond between us.

Our facilitator was part of our team, and she joined in the talk and told us her story. She wasn't personally familiar with military life, but had contributed to the war scene by volunteering for the American Red Cross during the Vietnam War.

The next assignment I liked was one where we made a figure out of a piece of clay. Once it dried, we were to speak to the audience and say what inspired us to make that object. There was always a personal story behind every piece of art presented.

Later that day we were each given a white candle in a glass jar and were encouraged to dedicate it to someone or to an organization as we approached the person who was facilitating the retreat. This person put the candle on a table until everyone placed and dedicated his or her candle. Then we had a moment of silence. I dedicated it to those who are suffering from PTSD and other war memories.

The part of the retreat I enjoyed the most was the beating of the drums. I had kept some information in my long-term memory about the brain and ancient drums. Something happens when the brain feels the beat of the drums. The brain wave theta is awakened and that's when it helps the individual have supernatural encounters. This was fascinating to me. I wanted my brain to experience something in the supernatural that day so that I may get some healing that night.

The last day we were taken to a fire pit and were instructed to write something on a small piece of paper that we wanted to get rid of such as anger, bitterness, and hatred. It could also be illnesses like depression or habits that are not healthy for us, physically or spiritually. One by one we approached the fire, turned in the thing we were giving up and destroyed it forever.

Learning about St. Francis

This retreat was the introduction to the healing process for my spirit and soul. We learned about St. Francis, a war veteran who became a P.O.W. He most likely suffered from PTSD. This interested me because I finally found someone I could relate to who had been through what I had experienced and also was a person of the Christian faith. I learned of the struggles he had when he attempted to assimilate to the civilian life his father wanted for him. His heart was heading toward a different direction than that of a prestigious merchant like his father. St. Francis had no motivation to take on the family business.

What I understood from this retreat was that St. Francis was searching for something deeper and bigger than himself. That's what motivated him to approach Pope Innocent III to begin the Franciscan Order.

The activity I enjoyed the most during this retreat was when we gathered in a circle under a ramada and were instructed to give our neighbor a piece of salmon. When we were all fed, we took turns putting anointing oil, frankincense from Israel, on each other's foreheads as we touched our neighbor's forehead to our forehead. The next step was we prayed for each other for healing.

I really was blessed to be part of this retreat and a lot of healing took place. My favorite activity was when we put oil on each other foreheads and then prayed for someone in the group. For me, the most important thing about the anointing oil is that, it goes straight to the nerves. It's very powerful!

Pilgrimage

The pilgrimage from Assisi to Rome was a success in my healing journey. I went with a group that facilitates this program which sends veterans yearly on this pilgrimage. We visited the Vatican the second day we were there, and it was a breath-taking moment for all of us. But I didn't receive any spiritual moments that showed me God's glory. It was at another cathedral in Rome that I felt the presence of the Holy Spirit so strongly that I fell down prostrate. I was enjoying His visit when a crowd of Italian citizens approached me,, asking me in their language if I was feeling sick. I just kept saying the "Holy Spirit", the "Holy Spirit" and then someone said that if I didn't get up that they were going to call the first responders and the police. I couldn't get up, the Holy Spirit had arrested me. Finally after the second time I was told they were going to call the police, the Holy Spirit instructed me to get up, and I obeyed him.

It was at Laverna that I received a supernatural encounter with the Lord. I saw these beautiful iridescent lights that were flying all around me. The same type of lights that I would see when I was a child living in Mexicali, Baja California, Mexico. This was awesome because Laverna is the place where St. Francis received his stigmata. Therefore, this made a lot of sense to me. I was filled with awe and with so much joy in my heart that I couldn't contain it!

Washington D.C.

I joined a secular program that helps Arizona veterans heal from PTSD. According to the itinerary we were to check in at the Southwest Airlines ticket counter at 6 a.m. I was picked up by a girlfriend of one of the veteran participants. She and her veteran friend arrived at my house early, about 5:30 a.m. in the morning. My mother came with us to see me off. I was so thankful to this lady because she was also going to pick me up from the airport and take me home when the trip was over.

When we arrived at the airport area to check in, I was the only female veteran checking in. I was surrounded by mostly Vietnam veterans, and a handful of Iraq and Afghanistan War veterans. I didn't talk to anyone else, but I didn't try to be with the crowds gathered at the airport for this trip to Washington D.C.

There was plenty of food to munch on, and coffee to keep us awake. The volunteers present made sure we all had something to eat before we boarded the plane.

About ten minutes after I got there my roommate, Karen, arrived. She was a Vietnam veteran who was a nurse. I had already met her through a veteran program for which she serves as a board member. We met during the mandatory orientation meeting we attended months earlier.

We were ready to board the plane. As we walked in a single file line, we heard someone's voice announcing us as war veterans who had honorably served our country. Everyone in the airport began to cheer and clap. I felt so thankful and was a bit frightened at the same time that my legs almost went out on me. They felt so heavy, like I was wearing ten pounds of ankle weights.

We arrived at Washington Reagan Airport and were bussed to the hotel. Once we were all settled in our rooms, we gathered to go visit the Vietnam Memorial. I didn't understand too much about the memorial, and it didn't make sense to me because I'm not from that war era. Some of the veterans from the Vietnam War began to share, and most of them had never spoken about their war experiences before. These veterans were letting go of some of the hurts they had been holding on for decades. It was an honor to be in their presence.

The next day we visited the World War II Memorial, and then we revisited the Vietnam Memorial. It wasn't until we were taken to the Arlington National Cemetery that I was in awe. We had a tour guide who drove us around in a bus and would stop along the way, so we could see some of the tomb stones of famous people like the Kennedys up close.

We also were blessed to see the changing of the marine who guards the tomb of the unknown soldier. It was such an awesome experience. It's one thing to watch this on t.v. but to view it in person is breath taking. This trip made me fall in love with the fact that I did serve my country. I was part of the most powerful military in the world.

We finally arrived at the hotel, had dinner and took a break before our evening session. Since the men had shared the night before, and it was a success, more men continued to talk about how they were feeling about holding on to memories that involved the Vietnam War. These thoughts were issues they wanted to release and that's what took place that night. There were many tears that left the eyes of some of those warriors. I just saw that tissue box travel from war veteran to war veteran. There was so much healing taking place that night!

On Saturday, November 11, we were invited to view a section of the Pentagon. When we arrived, we waited in line to receive our visitor badges. Once we were cleared, we were escorted in by a security guard who took us to several different sections.

I was fine until I saw a portrait of the Twin Towers being blown up by the airplane that crashed into it. being piloted by the terrorists who hijacked the plane. I began to get emotional and teary eyed. I told one of our professional counselors I might need some help during the tour. I was able to keep my composure but then we were taken to the chapel. That's when I began to cry. My eyes were filled with tears, and I kept wiping my face with my hands as they collected my tears. The counselor that I had spoken with earlier came to me and sat next to me.

The tour was over after we were taken to see the memorial for the victims who died as a result of the tragedy.

I boarded the bus to return back to the hotel, but one of the counselors told us that two of the counselors were staying back with some Iraq and Afghanistan War veterans who wanted to stay back. This was our memorial. I asked to stay back with my brothers and sister. I was given authorization and left the bus to join my peers.

A female counselor approached me and asked me how I was doing, and I began to be transparent. I told her, with tears in my eyes, as I looked at the Pentagon building, that it was my fault that it happened. Then she asked me why. I told her I had a premonition about the tragedy, but because of fear I didn't reveal it to anyone. I began to let her know about how I was treated in the army for being a faithful Christian, and all the things my superiors had put me through. I told her most of my peers also bullied me because I wasn't behaving like they were or living my life like they were outside of their military uniforms.

It took a while though before I trusted her to have the courage to tell her exactly what was going on in my mind and heart. This was something that was weighing heavy in my heart. It was one of the reasons why I had been suffering for many years from PTSD. But that day something happened when I let it all out, and there was someone who was not a church individual who heard my story and did actually hear me and listened to me. I felt like a weight was just lifted off from me, and it was never going to return. It was a great feeling. I was so blessed to have been part of the program.

When we arrived in Phoenix, we were surprised. We were taken to a hotel for a reception, but when we entered a room it was all decorated and our families and friends were there cheering us on. It was a welcome home celebration!

I saw my mother, one of my brothers and his girlfriend. They were yelling my name and waving the U.S. flag. I also saw many wonderful people who I have worked with in a veteran's ministry here in the valley. I also saw a couple of the local news media channels were filming the event to show on the nightly news.

That night every single veteran was recognized. A family or friend came to the front where there was a microphone, and said the name of his or her veteran. When the veteran stood, everyone cheered and clapped. Then the person behind the microphone spoke about his or her hero. Each individual had the opportunity to speak about the veteran in his or her life.

This was the welcome home that some veterans had never received. Once again this moment was a needed event in a war veteran's life, especially for the Vietnam War veterans who were actually mistreated when they returned from the combat zone.

What program would you like to participate in?

Did you like that program?

What was the program like?

Other Illnesses

We all have three elements regardless of what our ethnic background, religious beliefs, and social status. We have a physical body, a spirit and a soul. When one is hurting or not complete, we are not whole. For instance, the body functions and has five senses, nerves, a brain, organ and cells. Our soul has personality and consists of a conscious mind (thinking/reasoning), will (choices), subconscious mind, emotions (memories/ feelings) and (beliefs and attitudes).

I was diagnosed with diabetes in the army in the summer of 2004. One day when I went to use the restroom I felt real weak and passed out. When I regained consciousness, I told one of my superiors what happened to me, and he sent me to the clinic on post to get examined. After several tests were done, there was a positive report for diabetes type two. I was given all the information on how to take care of myself from the medication that I was going to receive to how to check and monitor my blood sugar daily. Plus, I had to eat healthy and exercise regularly, which was something that I already was doing.

Now that I was a civilian with diabetes, I didn't manage to control it as I was taught in the army. My health care provider requires me to take tests every three months to check the level of my blood sugars. My levels have been a bit high at times so my physician prescribed an additional medication to take to help lower my blood sugar. It didn't work for me because the new medication lowered my blood sugar too low, and it would cause for me to call the first responders. It would take several years before my doctor would be able to find a new medication for me.

I had the option of taking cooking or exercise classes, and I chose to sign up for exercise cases at the V.A. Hospital to help with lowering my blood sugar levels. I felt better when I exercised. I knew that this was one of the key components to my healing process from PTSD and depression.

Sleep Apnea

Around 2005, during my driving time from Luke's Air Force Base on my way home I began to get real sleepy and often fought to stay awake. As I was driving north on Dysart Road and made a complete stop at a stop sign, I began to get even more sleepy. There were times when it was difficult to keep driving with my eyes wide open. I struggled to keep them opened. I kept yawning. I knew there was something wrong with my health and believed it was because my sugar levels were elevated. But when I arrived home, I immediately checked my blood sugar levels, and they were not even high.

After some time, I decided to seek my health care provider and told her what was going on. I explained to her it wasn't the diabetes, and asked if she could check to see if it was another chronic condition causing the sleepiness.

She began to ask me some questions and after a long list of inquiries she discovered it was very possible I had sleep apnea. The most obvious question was did I snore during my sleep, and I had to answer with a yes. She made an appointment with a specialist. That's exactly what was going on with my body. I had sleep apnea and was losing about eleven breaths per minute during my sleep.

Chronic Back Pain

In 2009 while I was at a Bible study at the men's Recovery Home, I began to get real sick. The back pain was so unbearable that I could only take baby steps when I walked. I wanted to cry because I was hurting. Suddenly the pain creeped up on me and went up another notch. I was now hurting more than before. I decided to call 911 and have the ambulance come for me. I told someone in leadership what happened. I gave someone my car keys and told them a family member would be coming by to pick up my car.

When the paramedics arrived, someone from my church told them I had excruciating pain due to a past fall. The first responders put me on a gurney and took me to the Phoenix V.A. Hospital because I told them that I was a veteran. I heard someone call my pastor's wife. She got on the phone and told me she would be praying for me. I was transported to the hospital.

When I arrived there, I was crying because I was in so much pain I couldn't stand it any longer. I wanted to get rid of the pain. I was so desperate and didn't care anymore on how it was going to go away. I didn't care what medication I was going to be administered as long as I wasn't going to be suffering anymore.

After waiting for a couple of hours, I was given some medication via an intravenous needle, and the pain rapidly left my entire body. I was so relaxed, I fell asleep.

Migraines

In the spring of 2013, I was living alone in my apartment in Phoenix when I began to suffer from migraine headaches. It was approximately 9 p.m. during the week. I didn't want to call my family members because they were all getting ready for bed to get ready for work the next day. I didn't want to call a taxi because I was disoriented, and I couldn't trust a stranger to drive me to the hospital. I was really ill and began to vomit, leaving some samples on my kitchen wall. It got very ugly in my apartment that night.

After nearly three hours of agony, I decided to call 911 because I felt like my head was going to burst into two pieces and my brain would splatter all over the apartment. It was very serious pain, and I wanted some help to alleviate my torture. Once the paramedics arrived and I identified myself, they put me on the stretcher and took me to the nearest hospital. This time I wasn't transported to the Phoenix V.A., although I had requested that they transport me there. They refused and took me to their choice of hospital.

Everything Kept Spinning

I had heard about vertigo and the symptoms people experience were briefly explained to me. It happened to me in early 2018, and it wasn't something that I could describe in detail. The best way to speak about it is similar to when I got off of a ride at an amusement park, and I felt like I was still on the ride. With everything spinning and feeling there was no end. This was not only the scariest feeling, but it was also the strangest of all illnesses to have.

My younger brother drove me to the Phoenix V.A. Hospital, and I checked in the emergency department. My mother was also there with me to hold on too because I couldn't stand up straight. I was out of balance so once I was registered, I was placed in a wheelchair.

I was taken to the back and put in a room right away. It wasn't even long before I was given some medicine via an I.V. Within half an hour I was feeling so much better. The doctor on call prescribed some medication for nausea and vertigo to take in the future should it happen again after I was discharged. I was given instructions on how to administer the medication and was told to follow up with my primary care physician. The only thing I could do after my discharge was to rest and take a long break.

Do you have a physical illness that slows you down?

It's possible some of those physical ailments came into your body as a result of a trauma you have suffered. I had an idea that wouldn't leave my mind until I sought out an answer. My thought was, from my own experience, that traumas did affect my physical body and slowed down my body in so many ways. It was during one of my primary care physician visits I did my inquiry and, to my surprise, my doctor confirmed I was correct. Most of our physical weaknesses derive from mental abuse and or traumas that have entered into our lives.

Don't give up, the good news is that God is in the business of healing.

> *Bless the Lord, O my soul and all this is within me. Bless his Holy name! Bless the Lord, O my soul, and forget not all his benefit, who forgives all your iniquity, who heals all your disease.*
>
> Psalm 103: 1-2 (NIV)

Good Samaritans

I was deeply depressed because I wanted to have quality time to visit my daughter each time I would drive from Phoenix to Long Beach. But during that moment in my life it never happened because her father would limit the time I could spend with her by making plans with her. He was extremely possessive of her although she was of legal age. He used the excuse she lived under his roof to manipulate and control her. There was nothing I could do about it, and because of his treatment of her, I became very sad and vulnerable.

I wanted to do something to help her, but I was helpless. The only thing I could do was to pray to my God that one day it wouldn't be this way and I would make up the lost time with my one and only daughter.

I would attend church although I was very depressed and had a disturbed spirit and mutilated soul. There was one occasion after the service was over, and I was leaving the ladies room and began to cry. I told one of the sisters that I just wanted God to end it all for me. I continued to ask God to just end my life. The sister hugged me real tight and began to pray for me. As soon as she began to intercede for me, I began to cry more and released everything that was hurting me. After she finished with those powerful words that were aligned to God's Holy Scriptures, I felt at peace and stopped crying. My spirit was calm, and my soul wasn't disturbed as much. I thanked her for her quick actions to meet my spiritual needs, which grounded me and gave me a peaceful spirit.

I got real sick one day in 2009 after church service, and I couldn't drive myself home. My pastor's wife had one of the sisters drive my car home, and she followed us. I was so weak I couldn't drive, but I wasn't going to let that stop me from worshipping the Lord; from loving Him and serving Him. I was blessed to have leadership who cared about me and was willing to go the extra mile to make sure I made it home safe.

A Good Friend

I had a friend named Reverend Nancy, who was a positive influence in my life. She knew pretty much everything going on with me. She was always speaking life into me. When I was going through some serious things in my life, she recommended that I put on some worship music on and start praising the Lord in my apartment.

Reverend Nancy was a seasoned woman of God who cared about me. She was worried about me at one time in my life because I was going through a trauma I had experienced in a Christian church. She prayed for me to forget everything that ever took place in that church.

Her prayers were so powerful that one day I woke up and didn't remember my past. I began going through photographs and didn't remember taking them. I looked at family photos, and they all seemed like strangers to me because I couldn't recall anything that had happened for the past twenty years. I began telling people that I had lost my memory and, at one point, I told some people that I had a double personality.

I approached Reverend Nancy about it, and she told me that the reason I couldn't remember was because she had prayed for me to forget about all the hurt and memories that had occurred to me in the church. Her prayers were so dynamic they made me forget many things about my past. Once I found this out, I began to pray to the Lord and asked Him to help me get my memory back because I wanted to heal from all my past hurts. That's exactly what took place after I finished praying.

Grocery Store Manager

Another person who is part of my brigade is a manager at a supermarket. One day I was grocery shopping, and I was triggered by something I don't recall at this time. I was feeling unsafe and frightened. I needed to be alone and was very disoriented. I knew that I was in no condition to drive myself home. I immediately asked an employee if I could speak with the manager. When he approached me, I introduced myself and told him that I was a war veteran who suffered from PTSD and, at that moment I was having a PTSD moment. I told him how I was feeling, and I just needed to stay in a quiet place where I could feel safe so I could calm myself. After I began to feel safe, I would be able to drive myself home. He honored my request and had me sit in an office away from everyone else and asked one of his female employees to stay with me until I felt better and was ready to leave the store. I eventually felt safe, went to my car and drove home. That was the end of that day.

Lost in a Hardware Store

A person that I will also always remember is the manager of a hardware store I went one day to shop for some material for a woodworking project I had committed myself to creating and finishing.

This time I was triggered by men. It was the fact I was surrounded by men that I began to feel unsafe in the store. I asked a female employee if she could get a female supervisor to come and speak with me. She was nice about the situation and went to find one for me. In the meantime, I was feeling like I was all alone in a room and the walls were closing in on me. I experienced anxiety at a different level. I remembered how, at times, when I was in the army I was the only female in the room, and sometimes it was a very uncomfortable feeling.

When the female supervisor came to the area, I briefly explained what was going on with me. She had me sit in an area of the store with a female employee. She told me I could stay there until I felt better. She said if I needed someone to walk me to my car to let her know so that she could arrange it.

After some time, my PTSD moment faded, and I began to feel better. I finished my visit to the store by making my purchase and quickly exiting.

Triggered on the Freeway

There was a time in 2013 when I was returning from California to Phoenix, and I was triggered because I saw a Middle Eastern man wearing a turban. I immediately went to Iraq in my mind. I went into PTSD full -blown mode and got lost on the 605 N. Freeway. I was searching for the entrance to the 1-10 East, but because I got lost and was experiencing PTSD, I didn't know exactly what I should do. The only thing I thought of doing was calling 911 and explaining to them who I was, what was going on, and what I needed. I told the lady on the other line that I was an Iraq War veteran who suffers from PTSD, on my way home from Long Beach to Phoenix, and I needed to find the 1-10 East Freeway. Once I accomplished finding the freeway entrance, I would be fine.

The operator kept me on the phone and was very compassionate and professional about the entire situation. She is one of my many angels who have helped me to become the strong and resilient woman of God that I am today. Like so many who have played a part in my life, big or small, I'm eternally grateful to everyone who has helped me along the way toward my healing journey from depression and PTSD.

National Holiday

My mother worked at a hospital in Phoenix in the housekeeping department. I lived near the hospital and decided one day to meet her in the cafeteria for lunch. But, I got triggered when I saw some patriotic decorations. I saw some small U.S. flags adorning the cafeteria along with the U.S. patriotic colors, red, white and blue. The scene brought me back to Iraq when the dining facility was decorated during our Fourth of July celebration out in the war zone. This was also a time when we were celebrating a national holiday. Before I knew it, I was back in Iraq and feeling unsafe. I quickly approached a lady in scrubs and asked if she was a nurse. She verified she was. I briefly explained to her who I was and what I was doing there. I asked her to please help me find my mother as I gathered my lunch onto my tray. When I finished putting all my food on the tray, I was about to pay for my lunch. She told the cashier she was going to use her employee credit to pay for both of our lunches. She invited me to sit with her and her co-workers, but then I spotted my mother. I thanked her for everything.

I went to meet my mother and explained to her what had happened to me. I told her that the nurse was real compassionate, didn't judge me, and even paid for my meal.

A Bank Visit

Sometime in 2016, I went to make a transaction at my local bank and had no idea that I was going to get triggered. I began feeling uncomfortable when I was in line. It felt like the temperature went up a notch, and I began to sweat. It was definitely not a good feeling. Soon after I became tense and, before I could blink my eyes I was taking a journey to Iraq, but I didn't quite make it because I first spoke with a young banker, sitting at a desk. I approached him and identified myself to him. Then I briefed him on what was going on with me.

A female customer had been listening in on our conversation and came to me and asked if she could help because she was a licensed counselor. I said all I wanted was to sit down and made it clear to them that I didn't want to hurt myself or others. I just wanted to sit and wait until I was coherent. I needed to calm myself before I left the bank to drive myself home.

They were both very compassionate with me and the young banker went ahead and honored my request. He said that I could sit in the waiting area and eat some chocolate candies he had given me. I stayed until I felt safe. Once I was back to feeling better, I was able to drive myself home.   But first, I went to his office to thank him for taking good care of me and not judging me.

Who has been a good Samaritan in your life?

How did he or she help you get through your day or moment?

• 138 •

Successful Moments

My dream to finish my higher learning finally was completed in September, 2007. I graduated from Wayland Baptist University with a bachelor's of science degree in Biblical Studies and a minor in Office Technologies. During that time, I was also enrolled in several classes in two Maricopa Community Colleges to fulfill my general education requirements for my degree with WBU. I traveled to different locations for the classes because not all of them were held at the university. One professor held her class at a junior high school and another at his home church. I drove all over the valley and enjoyed it.

I was active in a coalition that brings awareness and educates the community about domestic violence and sexual assault. I was selected various times to share my testimony to students at a local university who were in the social work and or mental health program. They wanted to learn from someone who had been in an abusive relationship or was a sexual assault survivor.

Each time that I shared my testimony, it helped me to get my voice back and to establish my spirit in the place where it should be. It was a long process, but it helped a tiny bit. Although it didn't heal me, it made me a more mature woman, and it gave me a purpose in life.

My Story on T.V.

There were other times when I was in front of a camera telling my story like the day when I was interviewed by a local government channel doing a series on domestic violence in October for Domestic Violence Awareness Month. I was invited to share with the public about my experience with my abuser and all the horrible things that he did to me. I made sure to tell about my past, but also my present life, what I was striving for now and that I no longer was in an abusive relationship.

The Brick Paver Ceremony

While living in low-income housing for veteran women, someone sponsored me to have my name placed on a brick paver at the Anthem Veteran's Memorial Park. On November 3, 2015, we arrived at the park to have the honorary bricks placed. It *was* an honor and a privilege to be part of such a ceremony and event. I was blessed to have my family witness this take place. It was a double blessing to have my daughter with me sharing this moment.

During my stay at the veteran women's home, the director was partnering with a college to bring a humanities program to the complex. She selected a few veteran women and other women who were related to military personnel. We started out with fourteen women, and only seven graduated. I was one of the seven who completed the entire program. The classes we studied were: Art, U.S. History, English, Philosophy and Ancient Writings.

Writing is Therapeutic

A lot of healing took place when I wrote my first book *From Baja to Baghdad and Back to the Barracks*. This book is about my military experience, and it's a faith-based story. I let the readers know about everything; like I did not want to get fired from the army when I was ill, but they wanted to get rid of me.

Then I suffered two traumas, and the last one ended my career. But there's a secret in this story that I reveal to the readers. It has to do with a man everyone was looking for during the Iraq War, but no one could find him. Then God told me in a dream where he was hiding and gave me specific instructions to give to Military Intelligence. Within a month and a half, they found this infamous man. He was hiding in a spider hole.

I had to obey the Lord and risk being seen as a terrorist or enemy of the U.S or even looked upon as a mentally ill soldier who was making things up. I risked so much, but in the end the Lord took care of everything for me. Now that my book has been published, I don't carry that weight anymore. I feel free!

I first tried to write a manuscript with Amazon, but I wasn't having any luck and made many mistakes. After several months of failing and learning and failing some more, I added to my knowledge about writing a book. I began to develop a new kind of confidence in myself. I ordered some copies and began to edit them myself. When I noticed that I still needed professional help, I decided to hire a publisher

I selected a Christian publishing company, and within a couple of weeks they accepted my manuscript. The process of publishing my first book began. I had the liberty to request changes as often as I wanted. At one point there were no more changes being made to the manuscript, so it was time to end my contact with the editing department. The book then went to the next phase of the publishing process. It continued and was approved through the distributors, Amazon, and Barnes & Noble's online.

During the same time the first book was being published, I was writing my second book, Chasing Dragonflies about my domestic violence testimony. I had time to self-publish that one through Amazon because I had already learned so much from writing my first book that the second one come naturally to me. Although I have only sold two books so far, I'm rejoicing because I wrote my story and it's now available to the public.

The Three Heart Award

I was active with the Arizona Coalition to End Sexual and Domestic Violence (ACESDV) and was selected on various occasions to speak about my experience of abuse to mental health students at local universities and to others in the community.

I was the recipient of the Three Heart Award from the ACESDV in May, 2016. I was required to make an acceptance speech. All I could think of was to briefly write about my life and thank those who have helped me along the way, because I love them also and thank God for them. The following is part of my acceptance speech:

"I have been through various seasons throughout my entire life and each time my emotions plummeted to the edge of the abyss and then reached the stratosphere. After my initial trauma at the age of six, I began to construct a barrier with yellow wallpaper. I became the poster child for abuse. And depression came into my life to the point that I scratched many pieces of that ugly wallpaper. During my young adult life, I was put on temporary antidepressants, which made matters worse. My emotions became cold like a winter storm that left ground temperatures and created black ice.

I wasn't fond of the side effects of these prescribed medications, therefore, I had a meeting with my soul to design a plan to rearrange my wallpaper and barrier. I was determined that society would no longer see me scratching that wallpaper by learning how to smile and wear a mask. In doing this I built my own Jerusalem wall and named it 'The No One is going to Hurt Me Wall'.

I designed shelves to store the various masks for different people and occasions. They helped me to camouflage the unhealthy emotions that were locked deep in the spring well of my life called the heart. This was my own prescription for depression and suicidal tendencies.

This barrier was not a success, because I kept getting hurt. Therefore, I decided it was time to rebuild the wall and give it a different name. The first thing that I had to do was to let go of the masks that I had on the shelves. I took them to the altar one day and burned them because I wanted to please God with the aroma of my ugliness being damaged and completely destroyed by the combustion.

I knew that the burning of such fabrics like cotton, polyester, canvas and silk would be a sweet smell to his nostrils. I then released the wrecking ball and it demolished the shelves so that I would not be tempted to replace any of the masks. Behind these masks I found many dreadful emotions and the one that stood out the most as anger. In the course of two decades I kept rebuilding my wall as I sought professional help and continued to search for God's character. I noticed that as I drew closer to him, my wall began reparation at a more efficient pace than when I had attempted to continue relying on my own intelligence, knowledge and wisdom.

Today I have the emotional intelligence that I was desiring to achieve for so many years. And as I look back and recall all those masks that I wore, I would not change any of my experiences. My testimony is what has cultivated me to be the humble and resilient soul that I am today. When individuals see me face to face, I believe they see a genuine woman with many virtues such as righteousness, morality, integrity and dignity to name a few. I'm a success because people have invested time in me and believed in me. There have been many nice humanitarians that have changed my spiritual diapers. I'm extremely grateful for each and every individual that has been a part of my life. And in return, I long to have the opportunity to continue helping others in the same way; those who have had a life with yellow wallpaper that has disabled their spirits and left them with mutilated souls. For this reason. I have re-named my version of the Jerusalem Wall; it's called the 'Peace and Love Wall'.

I'm content and very proud of my accomplishments because they give me hope to continue living. It's important to have a mission in life and, as a veteran, I truly understand that I can't live without a mission. But most important, I can't exist without God in my life."

What success, triumphs or fond memories have you had in your life lately?

A Message from the Author

I have received a lot of kind words and positive moments from so many people that have been in my life during my struggles with PTSD and MST. Everyone's gestures have helped fuel my spirit and soul to the place where I am today. I find myself in a very steady and grounded atmosphere. I'm proud to be all that God has created me to be and then some. I'm eternally grateful to my civilian brigade for all of their love, compassion and support. God bless each and every one of you for what you have done for me because today I'm part of the twenty-two a day minus one!

About the Author

Maria Gastelum is a Certified Community Chaplain through Church for the Nations in Flagstaff, Arizona. Her place of worship is Victory Outreach East Phoenix. She lives in Phoenix, and has one daughter, Tatiana Shellman.

Maria received a bachelor's of science in Biblical Studies from Wayland Baptist University Plainview Texas (Phoenix Campus) in September, 2007. She is a U.S. Army Iraq War Veteran, serving in two major deployments: Operation Desert Springs 2002 after the 9-11 tragedy; and Operation Iraqi Freedom 2003. Maria is also the author of From Baja to Baghdad and Back to the Barracks and Chasing Dragonflies.